Home Poultry Keeping

Second edition

Dr Geoffrey Eley MA

D1461334

A & C Black • London

Acknowledgements

Tom Newbould MSc, BA (Hons) for new sections, updates and photographs on pp. 25-6, 52-60, 67, 68-70

Paul Chapman for illustrations on pp. 53, 54, 55, 57, 58, 65, 66, 67.

With thanks to exhibitors at the Ulster Poultry Federation, James Worsley, Miss A Straughan and Mr G Marston for allowing their birds to be photographed.

Second edition 2002
Reprinted 2003, 2004, 2005

A & C Black Publishers Ltd
37 Soho Square, London W1D 3QZ
www.acblack.com

© 2002 A & C Black Publishers Ltd

ISBN 0 7136 6319 7

All rights reserved. No part of this publication may be reproduced or used in any form or by any means – graphic, electronic or mechanical, including photocopying, recording, taping or information storage and retrieval systems – without the permission of the publishers.

A CIP catalogue record for this book is available from the British Library.

A & C Black uses paper produced with elemental chlorine-free pulp, harvested from managed sustainable forests.

Typeset in 11 on 13pt Rotis Serif

Printed in the United Kingdom by Biddles Ltd
King's Lynn, Norfolk

Contents

Health and Pleasure

For over 2000 years poultry have been kept in Britain and for an even longer span in the Mediterranean lands. Today, domestic poultry keeping is both a worthwhile hobby and an outstanding contributor to the ideal of home self-sufficiency. Eggs contain carbohydrates, fats and proteins, essential vitamins and minerals – including iron, a vital constituent of healthy blood.

Apart from the strong appeal of producing at least some of one's own food, often the responsibility for the care of a domestic poultry unit is given to younger members of the family and this can be a rewarding experience for young people. It fosters a basic knowledge of livestock management, simple biology and the processes of life, and competent record keeping. Even discipline comes into it – keeping poultry is a seven-day-a-week job, with such daily chores as feeding, watering and egg collecting.

Even if you have only limited space, as few as six well-managed hens will keep a family in eggs. With the cost of the necessary concentrated feedstuffs (and, remember, laying birds cannot thrive on household scraps alone) you will not show much cash profit from poultry keeping on a small scale – but you **will** have better quality and fresher eggs than any you can buy, as well as enjoying an absorbing hobby.

There are some 'sideline' profits to be had from domestic hens. Not the least of these is your own supply of poultry manure, a highly concentrated fertiliser for garden or allotment. In addition, surplus birds can often provide meat for the table.

Basis of Success

Domestic poultry can lay between 150 and 200 eggs per bird each year. This is an average of three or four eggs from each bird in a week – but do not expect their contribution to be as regular as this since the birds usually lay most heavily in the Spring and more spasmodically in the late Autumn. To achieve this level of egg production at home there are certain principles to be grasped. These include:

- Keeping only first-class pullets which have been selected and bred to lay (you are unlikely to find these in the market, so buy from a reliable poultry breeder).
- Providing enough properly balanced food to produce eggs.
- Ensuring your poultry house can be kept dry, is easily cleaned and kept hygienic.
- Separating pullets from any yearlings or second-year birds (older hens often harass young stock and stop them getting enough food).

There is no reason why poulty keeping should be hard work or make you feel like you cannot leave for a weekend. By planning housing requirements and other matters carefully from the outset you will avoid this happening.

Good Housing

The initial cost of a good housing system is unavoidably high, largely because timber is now expensive, but it will be fully repaid in high egg yields over many years – and even if you gave up the hobby the second-hand value of sound poultry houses can be substantial.

Although hens dislike mud and wind they can stand cold weather; they will even lay right through the coldest spell if they are properly managed – that is, protected against wind and given plenty of food and unfrozen water. Therefore the essentials of housing requirements are: dry feet and litter and all the fresh air possible without draughts.

When selecting a site for your poultry house consider the soil drainage, air movement, location of the dwelling house and the water supply. Remember there is the possibility of problems such as smells, flies, rats and mice. Good soil drainage ensures dry floors which will help prevent wet litter, dirty eggs, disease, and other problems.

If possible, the poultry house should be located where the prevailing summer winds will not carry smells towards your house, or those of neighbours.

A site on relatively high ground with a south or south-east slope and good natural drainage is best. The location of a poultry house at the foot of a slope where soil or air drainage is poor, or where seepage occurs, is unwise.

Fig. 1 A practical poultry shed and scratching run

If the house is located on a hillside, the site should be graded so as to carry surface water away from the building. In some instances, tile drains will be necessary to carry the water away from the foundation of the building adequately.

In winter weather, most of the windows should be in the front of the building; the house should face south to take advantage of the sunlight. The pen will be warmer, the litter drier and the birds more comfortable. The closed or back side of the house should provide maximum protection against the north-west wind. Where the prevailing winter storms are from the west, however, the house should face east.

The size of the poultry house will depend upon the type and number of birds to be housed, as well as the management system to be used. Different age groups and species of birds require different amounts of floor space for optimum results. In addition to the space needed for the birds, there should always be some additional space for storage of feed, supplies and equipment.

The removal of moisture from the building is one of the main problems in poultry keeping. The moisture in freshly voided manure is as high as 70 to 75 per cent, added to which there is the hens' respired moisture and further moisture from the in-coming air.

Good insulation of the poultry house will provide maximum bird comfort as well as helping to control excessive moisture.

Wood is Best

If you are buying a ready-made poultry house – and there are many good ones on the market, as shown in Figs. 1 to 5 – do make sure that the wood from which it is made is not too thin. Wood of this kind warps easily and is unable to withstand extremes of temperature; the result is a poultry house which is like an oven in summer and a refrigerator in winter.

Whatever type of house you buy or build for yourself, allow about 1 ft of area per bird, more if you choose hens of a large breed.

A very common mistake made by domestic poultry keepers is to provide the hens with only one earth or grass run. If possible, there should be at least two, to be used and rested alternately. This is the only way to avoid your

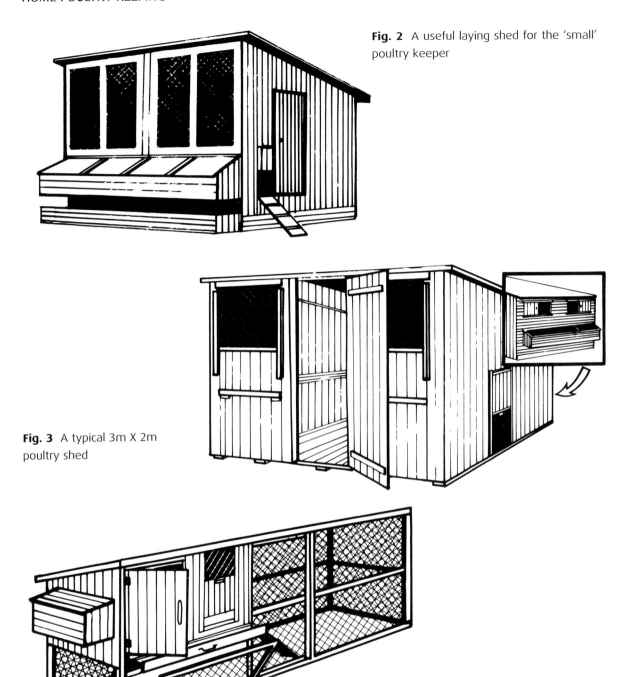

Fig. 2 A useful laying shed for the 'small' poultry keeper

Fig. 3 A typical 3m X 2m poultry shed

Fig. 4 'Hen pen' for limited space poultry keeping

Fig. 5 A slatted or wire-floored field laying house

poultry runs becoming a quagmire in winter and your birds looking, and indeed feeling, unhappy. If you have enough space the fold units shown in Fig. 6 are very convenient for moving about on grassland.

Where space is limited, poultry can be successfully kept by making use of a garden wall against which can be placed a covered run and small house (see Fig. 7). Such a covered-in scratching area can consist simply of wire netting sides with a roof sloping upwards to the top of the wall.

Advantages of the hen-pen are that it can be easily moved from one place to another and with its covered top, the scratching area is kept dry. The type of pen illustrated can be bought or made very simply, to a size of around 9 to 12 feet (3 to 4 m) long and $1^{1}/_{2}$ yards (1.5 m) wide – room for six or eight birds.

All types of poultry house can be greatly improved by covering the outside with felt – not the inside, as is sometimes done, because this only harbours insects and vermin. Regular creosoting or wood-staining your poultry house will help keep both it and the birds free from insect pests.

Fig. 6 Examples of movable fold units

Fig. 7 Lean-to on the wall of a house

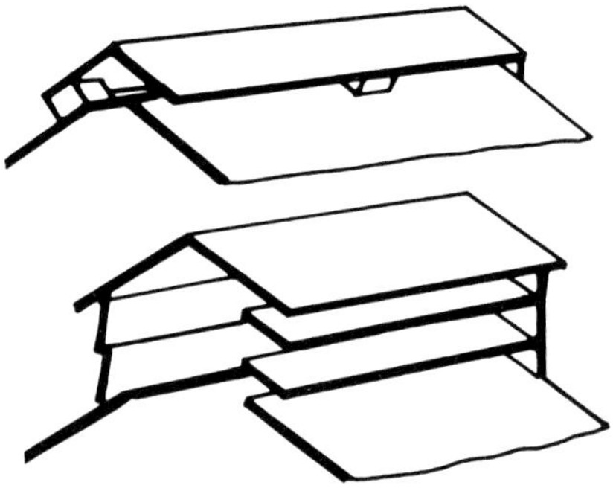

Fig. 8 Outlet ventilators for poultry houses

The Roof

The roof is a vitally important matter in poultry housing – it must fit extremely well otherwise you will be in trouble with damp.

If you are building your own poultry house, make sure the roof comes down over the eaves by at least 3 inches (75 mm) to carry off the rain. It is also helpful to have the roof guttered and allow the rain to drain off to a down spout and into water butts (providing you with a plentiful supply of rain water, so much better for the garden plants than tap water).

Cover the poultry shed roof with felt and put a generous quantity of tar on it once a year.

For permanent houses, corrugated iron lined with matchboarding $^1/_2$ inch (10 mm) thick, with a layer of felt between, makes, perhaps, the best possible kind of roof. It is expensive but has the merit of being warm in winter and cool in summer, and of course it lasts a very long time without attention.

If you decide on this kind of roof, allow a space of about 2 inches (40 mm) between the felt and the iron to allow a current of air to pass between.

Ventilation

Good ventilation is necessary to prevent birds suffering from respiratory diseases. It may sound surprising but poultry need over twice as much air as we do relative to their body weight! Inadequate ventilation causes a strong smell of ammonia and a simple test is a sniff when you feed the birds in the mornings – there should be no suspicion of 'fug'.

It is best to arrange ventilation from the front of the house (see Fig. 8) and if your house is, say, 6 feet (2 m) high, then the lower half, or slightly more, should be boarded up. Cover the top, open portion with fine mesh wire netting, fastened from the inside. Over this fix a light wooden frame fitted with glass – the idea is that you should be able to lower the glass frame to the bottom of the wire netting in hot weather or raise it nearly to the top when it is very cold. An alternative is to arrange the glass frames to open outwards at a slope, hinged at the top and bottom.

No such special ventilation windows are needed in a lean-to type of poultry house since the permanent open front is sufficient.

The Floor

There are probably three satisfactory ways of making a floor for your poultry house – boards, cement, or earth and gravel well beaten down:

1 **Boards** - well-tarred straight boards 1 inch (25 mm) thick should be used. Fit them close together and inside the foundations of the house itself. If they are closely fitted and nailed across a couple of stout battens, no damp will get in from below. It is **not** a good plan to construct the floor of your poultry house slightly larger than the house itself. Constructions like this, where the house itself stands on the larger floor area, mean that driving rain will most certainly penetrate during the winter.

2 **Cement** - while this has some merits – for example it is durable and permanent – the domestic poultry keeper must be careful that he uses sufficient depth of litter to avoid any ill effect that might otherwise accrue from such a hard, cold type of flooring.

3 **Earth or gravel** - be sure to mark out the site of the poultry house in dry weather (taking care that the hole lies square) and that surface soil is removed to a depth of about 5 inches (125 mm). The resulting hole should then be filled with good gravel, on top of which sufficient brick ends and similar rubble (clinkers would do) should be well pounded down until the hole forms a hard and level surface.

If a course of bricks is laid all round the outside so that the foundations of your house lie level upon them, and plenty of bedding is used inside, then this type of flooring is entirely satisfactory – except, perhaps, if the situation is very low lying, when rising damp could be troublesome.

Nest Boxes

Although nest boxes are not strictly necessary it is a good idea to allow one nest box (Fig. 9) for every three hens. Remember the hen likes to be sociable, although secluded, when she is laying, and the more warm bodies already in nest boxes the stronger is the hen's wish to force her way into the box!

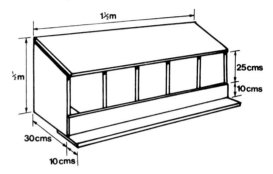

Fig. 9 Nest boxes constructed of plywood or 2 cm timber

Darkness is important. It tends to stop the birds eating the eggs, and the hen naturally chooses herself a dark spot in which to lay her eggs. If the nest box in your poultry house is exposed to full light, then cover it with a hanging piece of sacking.

It is preferable to place your nest boxes off the ground – but not at the same height as the perches in the hen house, otherwise the birds will roost in the nest boxes instead of on the perches. Litter the nest boxes with straw (rather than hay), wood shavings or sawdust.

Perches

Chickens have a natural instinct to perch, particularly at night which gives them some reassurance of safety. In the wild, this would

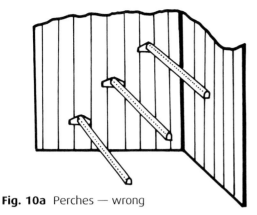

Fig. 10a Perches — wrong

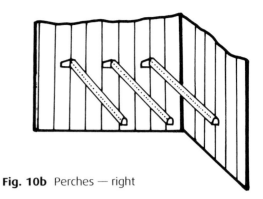

Fig. 10b Perches — right

help protect them from predators. Perches should always be level in terms of height to ensure the birds do not fight and quarrel for the highest positions.

Many small troubles of the poultry keeper can be traced to improper or defective roosting accommodation. By giving a little thought to the way in which the perches are arranged and fixed in your house, both loss and worry can be avoided (see Fig. 10). The best material for perches is timber of 3 inches (75 mm) thickness, with the top edges rounded off.

The most common error is overcrowding on the perches. Allow at least 8 inches (200 mm) perching space for each bird and you will not go wrong.

Another fault is to place your perches too high from the floor which leads to cut and sore feet, particularly in the case of heavy breeds, when they alight from such perches.

Never use poles or wood with the bark on. When the wood dries the bark becomes loose and the hollow space provides a grand retreat for thousands of undesirable insects. Neither should you leave any sharp edges if you use purchased timber to make your perches.

Hoppers

These are receptacles for poultry food or grit, usually kept under cover and so constructed that the birds can help themselves and, at the same time, further supplies keep coming down automatically from the reservoir above. If you use this kind of self-service hopper (Fig. 11) make sure the feeding stuff you are using does not clog up in the upper part of the hopper.

(See section on Feeding, page 27).

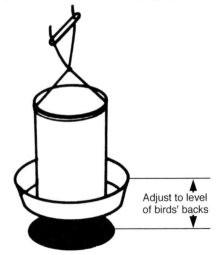

Adjust to level
of birds' backs

Fig. 11 Feed hopper

Building your Own

The house and run shown in Fig. 12 is designed to be built quite easily by the home handyman and to provide ample room for up to 12 well-managed birds. It is a design which has stood the test of time and is eminently practical, and the plan drawings give both Imperial and Metric measurements.

It will be seen from the illustration that the roosting house is raised 2 feet (.5 m) above the ground level. This serves three good purposes:

1 It provides additional space to the run;
2 It does not harbour rats and other vermin as houses do if built just off the ground;
3 The floor of the house provides shade from the sun during the summer.

Another feature is the position of the nest boxes in a detachable unit across the front of the structure. The position is not only easy for egg gathering but it is also the darkest part of the house, which the birds prefer for egg laying.

A door is provided at the side, but this position is optional. If there is not sufficient space for a side entrance, the nest boxes could be transferred to the side, and the door to the front; in which case it would be necessary to alter the general arrangement of the framework by shifting the window to either the right- or left-hand side of the front.

The small trap door between the house and the run is operated from the outside by means of a cord passing through a couple of screw-eyes fixed in convenient places in the side of the structure. This simple device saves the bother of entering the run every time the trap door has to be opened or closed. It is kept in the open position by placing the looped end of the cord over a rail.

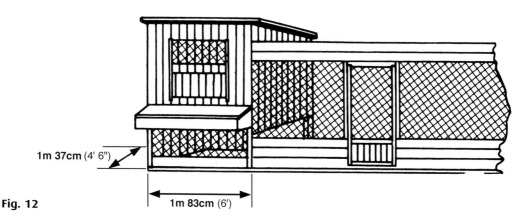

1m 37cm (4' 6")

1m 83cm (6')

Fig. 12

Size of House

The total length of the house and covered run is 18 feet (6 m); 6 feet (2 m) being the length of the house and 12 feet (4 m) that of the run.

This measurement is an arbitrary figure because the length of the run can either be reduced by about 2 feet (.5 m) or added to, depending on space available.

The covered run is simple enough, although it may be an advantage to add a hood in front, for further protection in bad weather. The height should be about 1 foot (.3 m) less than that of the roosting house, and the slope of the roof made to correspond.

The framework of this part is constructed of 2 inches by 2 inches (50 mm by 50 mm) section timber, and is covered with planed and rebated weatherboards at the back end and part of the front, while the top is covered with $1/4$ inch (5 mm) V-jointed tongued and grooved matching.

The roosting house is made in sections, each of which is framed with 2 inches by 2 inches (50 mm by 50 mm) timber, tongued and grooved V-jointed matched boards, about $6^{1/2}$ inches (150 mm) wide and $1/2$ inch (10 mm) thick are used for covering purposes.

Tongued and grooved floorboards 1 inch (25 mm) thick, placed across the narrow width of the structure, are used for the floor, and are purposely left loose for cleaning purposes.

The whole of the structure is supported on two 18 feet (6 m) lengths of 3 inches by 2 inches (75 mm by 50 mm) wood. This method of support will be found much more effective than placing the uprights on bricks, which can sink into the ground and upset the level of the structure. The legs of the house are held in position with small metal angle-brackets screwed to the legs and foundation plates.

Start by sawing up the timber for the framework for the house to the dimensions shown in the drawings (Figs. 13, 14 and 15). Mark each member as it is cut and keep the parts for each section in a separate pile to avoid confusion.

Assembling

Next, assemble the parts. This is quite a straightforward job, as the members are simply butted together and fixed with wire nails.

Having completed each sectional frame, fix the matchboards to the front section. Start at the right-hand end and fix the first board, allowing $1/2$ inch (10 mm) overlapping after having removed the tongue. The overlap covers the ends of the boards on the side section and consequently makes a neat flush finish when erected. A similar overlap is, of course, necessary at the other end.

When cutting the boards for the front section do not overlook the fact that the bottoms are fixed to the third horizontal rail and not the floor rail, as the space between these two members will be occupied by the nest box.

When fitting the boards, it is a good plan to cover the whole area and then cut out the window aperture with a saw.

Matchboard the back section in the same manner, not forgetting the overlap at each end. The boards of this section extend from the top of the frame to the bottom.

When all the sections are complete, give them a good coat of creosote or wood preservative on both sides and, whilst this is drying, start on the roof.

In the house described, the roof fits on top like a lid (see Fig. 16), the dotted line representing the tops of the walls of the house.

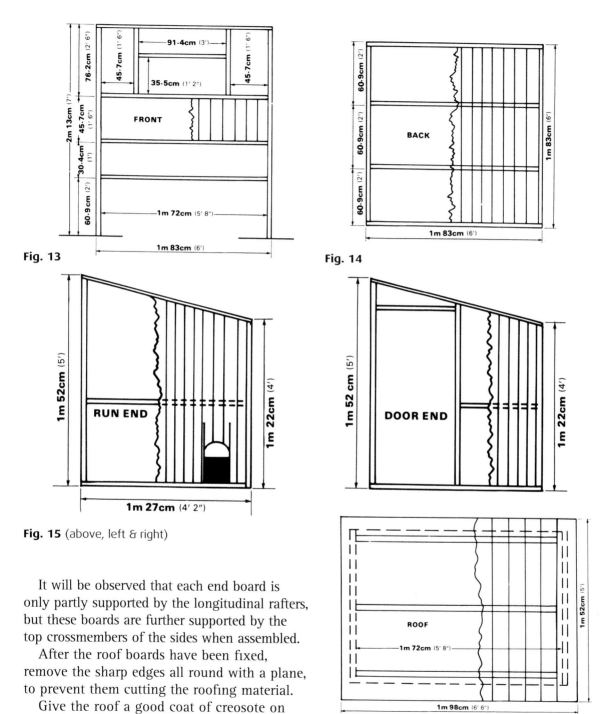

Fig. 13

Fig. 14

Fig. 15 (above, left & right)

Fig. 16

It will be observed that each end board is only partly supported by the longitudinal rafters, but these boards are further supported by the top crossmembers of the sides when assembled.

After the roof boards have been fixed, remove the sharp edges all round with a plane, to prevent them cutting the roofing material.

Give the roof a good coat of creosote on both sides.

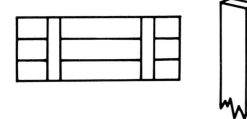

Fig. 17

The next procedure is to construct and fit the sliding shutter to the front section; details of this are shown in Fig. 17. The overall size of the shutter is 3 feet 4 inches long and 1 foot 6 inches wide (1 m by .5 m). It consists of matched boards held together by two vertical battens as shown. The shutter slides in rebates or grooves formed by nailing pieces of batten, 2 inches (50 mm) wide, over pieces half this width, and fastening to the front with screws.

The door is of simple construction, consisting of matched boards fastened to three ledges or battens. The length of the ledges should be ½ inch (10 mm) shorter than the total width of the door, to allow it to close against the doorstop.

When Help is Needed

When the holes for the fixing bolts have been marked and bored, the house is ready for assembly, but at least two people are needed to assemble.

When the four sections have been bolted together, test for squareness and vertical accuracy by means of a square and a plumb-bob. If correct, fit the roof, which is secured by driving screws through the bottom of the frame into the plate.

The Roofing Felt

Two 7 feet (2 m) lengths of standard width material will be required, which allows a little all round for turning under the edges and for an overlap at the horizontal joint in the centre of the roof. Start fixing at the front edge and work towards the back using galvanised clout nails.

Fold the overlapping portion neatly over and under the edges of the roof and fix it securely by nailing laths on the underside. Finish off the roof by nailing down the three battens – one in the centre and one at each end.

Floorboards

Cut and fit, but do not nail them down. Fix the door to its post and the door-stopping round the inside face of the frame. Make sure that the door closes properly against the stop and that the outside of the door is quite flush with the rest of the surface.

Now make the nest box as shown in Fig. 18 and fasten it to the structure by driving screws through the projecting ends into the two inside faces of the front uprights. The lid should be covered with roofing felt.

The Run

Mark and cut the front and back uprights and mark the exact positions for these on the foundation plates. The back uprights are spaced equally apart, while the front ones can be either arranged to allow the door to adjoin the roosting house, or in any other position, to suit the poultry keeper.

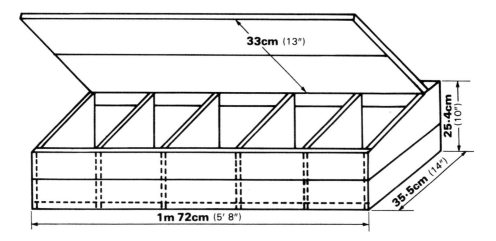

33cm (13")

25.4cm (10")

35.5cm (14")

1m 72cm (5' 8")

Fig. 18

Fix the uprights to the foundation plates by means of the iron brackets (using the same method as for the front legs of the roosting house). The front and back uprights adjoining the roosting house should be fixed to it with screws.

Carefully mark the positions for the tops of the uprights on the long, horizontal top pieces and then fix these members to the uprights with wire nails.

The next thing to do is to fix the cross pieces. These are placed squarely across the horizontals and fastened with nails, the ends being cut off flush with the front after fixing.

Proceed by fitting the rebated weatherboards to the back and side, starting just above the bottom of the foundation plate and working upwards towards the roof. (Test the long edges of the boards with a spirit-level from time to time to check any deviation from horizontal.)

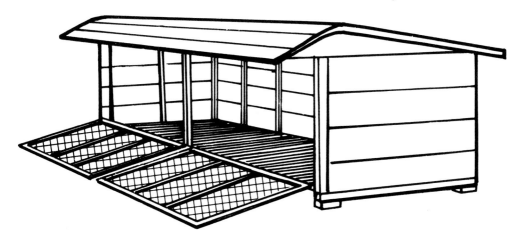

Fig. 19 A useful type of house raised off the ground on bricks or short legs and with a slatted floor.

Fig. 20 These two examples are easily moved and have a nest box which can be closed off when in use for chicks.

Fig. 21 Type of house used for colony poultry keeping in the open fields.

Saw the matched boards for the roof to length, and when securely fastened down give the whole structure a good coat of creosote.

Fixing the Door

The door is the next item to make. The best method is to use morticed and tenoned joints, but halved joints may be used at the top and bottom, and the middle rail fixed either with nails or screws. Another method would be to butt and screw the members together and reinforce the joints by using metal angle-plates.

Having completed the frame of the door, the lower portion should be filled in with matched boards.

Cross garnet hinges should be used for hanging the door which, of course, opens out-wards, and a thin strip of wood fitted to the inside face of the door post will prevent the door from being forced inwards and thus straining the hinges.

The wire netting may now be fixed to the inside faces of the framework, etc., and the door, using galvanised staples.

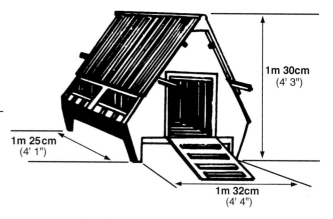

Fig. 22 In this ark model glass panels draw the birds in to feed inside, thus enabling shutting up to be done earlier in summer.

Fix the wire netting to the bottom part of the roosting house, fastening a short length of chain to the top of the front sliding shutter and a hook for its reception to keep the shutter closed. Screw in one or two screw-eyes for guiding the cord operating the trap door, and fit either turn-buttons or padlocks to the doors and nest box cover.

Other sound, well-tried types of poultry housing – all suitable for the home handyman to make – are shown in Figs. 19 to 24 inclusive.

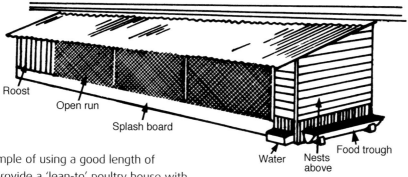

Fig. 23 An example of using a good length of garden wall to provide a 'lean-to' poultry house with covered run.

Fig. 24 Another good type of house; the design of the front allowing maximum light and air so that the house could be used intensively in winter without the birds coming out.

Fencing

One of the advantages of a **portable** system of housing is that the necessity for runs is dispensed with, so saving a considerable amount of expense and labour. When, however, space is limited and the fowls must be confined, then the best form of fencing is wire netting fastened to wooden posts. For most breeds of hens, fencing 6 feet (2 m) high is necessary – although, for the heavier breeds which are not so 'flighty', fencing of about 4 feet (1.5 m) is enough.

Do not buy cheap wire netting and also make sure that the mesh of netting is around 2 inches (50 mm). (The term mesh, used in connection with wire netting, means the space in between the wires.)

Keep it Neat

When wire netting 6 feet (2 m) high is used you will need wooden posts long enough to allow for driving them some 16 inches (.4 m) into the ground. The job is made easier if the stakes or posts are pointed at one end (and, of course, tarred or creosoted) so that they can be driven into the ground with a heavy hammer instead of having to dig holes for them.

Spare no pains to make your poultry fencing – and indeed the whole unit – look as neat and trim as possible (there is no reason why backyard poultry keeping need disfigure the surroundings but regrettably this happens, usually because rusty iron sheets, a hotch-potch of posts and other odds and ends have been used).

Dust Baths and Litter

Whatever kind of poultry house you use, its tenants must be provided with a dust bath – either inside or out.

The dust bath, as with wild birds, is essential to the well-being of your fowls. Not only does it help to keep them in healthy plumage, but it is also the only way birds can cool themselves in hot weather and get rid of insect pests.

In its simplest form a dust bath is a dusty place in the sun or around your poultry house where the birds can make their own pleasure. The nearest artificial equivalent is a heap of fine, dry soil or – better – a mixture of sawdust, dry earth, sand or road grit, kept in place by surrounding boards, and well sprinkled with insect powder.

If you have a fixed poultry house then provide the dust bath in a box, either inside the house or in a hole under the scratching shed. For up to 10 hens the box need be no more than 3 feet by $1\frac{1}{2}$ feet (1 m by .5 m) size.

Litter for Warmth

Litter not only provides the birds with exercise and diversion as they scratch for hidden corn – but it also maintains the birds' warmth and it forms a valuable part of manure for the garden. An ideal litter is wood shavings. Those from untreated wood are best and can often be purchased in compressed baled form.

It is important that the litter is kept dry and the birds will dust bathe in it.

Bark chippings can also be used in outdoor runs and have the advantage of decomposing over time along with the droppings to produce a good manure. However, they can only be used outside and as you will need to top them up and hose them down in order to get rid of the droppings, an effective drainage system is required.

An alternative form of litter is sand. Some people use sand on its own or mixed with a little gravel and it has the benefit of being able to absorb moisture well. Sand is dry without being dusty and it can easily be raked over, swept out and replaced. This type of litter also provides the birds with a good place to dust bathe.

Collecting Leaves

Using suitable litter for poultry need not be expensive. In the autumn, for instance, you can collect fallen leaves and store them. By winter they will be dry and ready to use. This makes an excellent litter and improves the organic quality of your poultry manure. An alternative is bracken fern which, if cut, harvested and stacked, is just as good as leaves and, incidentally, it makes a first class litter for your nest boxes since insects and other pests do not seem to like it.

The Way with Straw _____

Straw is commonly used in small houses and can be mixed with a little dry earth which seems to help the birds to break up the long straw.

All of these examples are suitable for utility poultry. If you are going to make a hobby of poultry exhibition, however, then you must be more selective in terms of litter – for instance the breeder of feather legged birds cannot allow his birds to scratch about in long litter since this would spoil the foot feather. Neither would the bantam breeder be able to litter his sheds with leaves which would nearly bury his pets! (See page 61 for a definition of bantams.)

Intensive Methods

The deep litter system and the built-up litter system are ways of housing poultry when the birds are confined for the whole of their lives and where litter is built up to a depth of between 6 inches and 10 inches (150 mm to 250 mm).

Bricks, concrete blocks, breeze blocks, and wood can all be used for building deep litter houses. If wood is used, it is best to line the entire inside with insulation material.

The intensive method of poultry keeping is not one often used by the small domestic poultry keeper. One reason for this, certainly in built-up areas, is the problem of obtaining an easy supply of sufficient litter at a reasonable price.

Where space is so limited as to prevent having adequate outdoor runs, it would possibly be better to consider laying batteries.

Battery Hens

This is the system most frequently used by commercial egg producers.

Although criticised by many quarters due to welfare concerns there are several reasons for

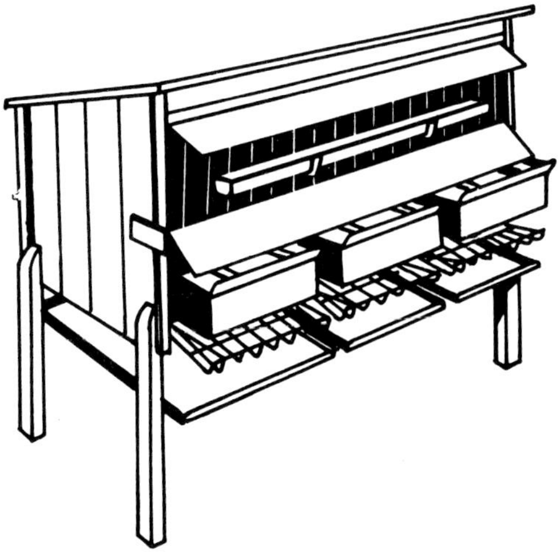

Fig. 25 A small-scale laying cage can be a most useful temporary home for laying hens whilst their main house is being 'spring cleaned' or repaired.

Fig. 26 Besides using laying cages inside another building, such as a shed or garage, a small unit can be placed against a wall (or stout hedge) — provided the cages are well roofed. Ideal for the 'back-yard' poultry keeper without a garden.

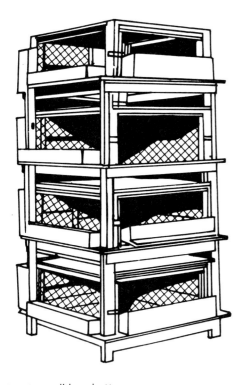

Fig. 27 A small hen battery

its popularity. Floor space requirement per bird is less, thus reducing the cost of housing per bird. The system also saves on labour in material handling.

One method is to provide only one cage per bird only; no heat or other apparatus is needed. A single bird laying cage is usually about 15 inches (.36 m) wide, and 18 inches (.5 m) in both depth and height. Alternatively you can design cages for more than one bird and with the exception of width, the other dimensions can be the same. The cages (Fig. 27) can be stacked in tiers but not more than four high and in 'units' from eight upwards, provided they have adequate protection from the elements.

Batteries are usually housed under cover for maximum egg yield, but they also give reasonable results sited out of doors, or in covered yards. In either case, hens are never let out. The main construction is of wire netting with a strong, woven netting floor through which the droppings fall to a false bottom in each tier of cages.

A food trough and a water container should be provided in front of each cage but no nest boxes are needed. As the floor is constructed with a slope of about 6 inches (150mm) per yard (1m), the eggs, laid on the wire floor, will roll out to an egg tray. The 'egg cradle' should extend about 7 inches (180 mm) beyond the cage front.

It must be stressed that even with an amateur's very small battery unit it is essential to allow adequate light and ventilation if the battery is under cover, and to keep the hen's quarters damp and vermin free.

Eggs of very high quality can be produced from birds kept in laying cages. But quality does depend very largely on the nutritional value of the food provided – the other factor governing egg quality is thought to be inherited. Birds fed on a ration deficient in vitamins A and B, and in such minerals as iodine and manganese, will probably produce eggs also poor in these nutrients.

Battery cages are in the process of being phased out over the next ten years with alternative cages, including perches, more room and dust bathing facilities.

Buying your Stock

Once you have chosen the type of poultry you will keep and made the decision about breed, variety, and colour, the next step is to lay the foundations of your flock. Depending on what you choose you have the option of purchasing hatching eggs, newly-hatched, growing, or adult stock.

The advantage of buying hatching eggs or newly-hatched young stock is that it is usually much cheaper. You will be able to see the birds grow and develop and they will immediately regard the place you give them as 'home'. You may also end up with stock of the same high quality as that which the vendor keeps! The disadvantage is that you will need to incubate the eggs in an incubator or under a broody and/or have the brooding facilities available for the chicks. With hatching eggs you have no way of predicting the ratio of males to females and it is unlikely that newly-hatched stock will be sexed.

If you are not buying hatching eggs, newly-hatched youngsters, or youngsters which are just 'off-heat', the three most important factors from your point of view are that (i) you obtain the best possible stock available within the range of your budget; (ii) that the birds are of an age before, within, or not too far past, their prime and will be capable of reproduction should you want to breed, and; (iii) that the birds are of optimum health, free from disease or parasites. For the beginner or inexperienced (and sometimes even experienced) poultry keeper this can be difficult and unfortunately there are many unscrupulous vendors out there who will readily accept your cash for poor birds! There are a number of things you can do to reduce the chances of being 'ripped-off' and help ensure you get an excellent foundation for your flock.

Step 1: Conduct research and contact organisations

The golden rule is to be patient and conduct some research. It is not advisable to go to a poultry auction, market, or show and purchase blindly without having done some research. Such places do, however, present an opportunity to see your preferred variety in the flesh – you may even change your mind! Be patient and remember that it is generally much harder to dispose of poor stock than buy them and, even though you will without doubt meet some pleasant people, many will have a vested interest in selling their breed or even their own stock to you!

An excellent way of finding out where to purchase quality pure-bred stock is to contact the relevant breed club (if it has one). Most of the popular varieties of chickens have a breed club which looks after the interests of the breed and may maintain a register of reputable breeders. There is a specialist Turkey Club in the UK and a few of the waterfowl varieties have their own clubs. There is an umbrella waterfowl and poultry club which will also steer you in the right direction.You can usually find the details of the clubs in the popular poultry magazines or on the best of the main poultry websites. We have made your task even easier by including a list of addresses in this book (see page 79).

Whoever you decide to contact can usually provide you with details of the best exhibition or utility breeders or those who may have stock suitable as pets. They may give you further information about the availability of your chosen variety and advise you on specific suitability. There is now even a website that will conduct and contact breeders on your behalf, presenting you with details of what is available. Bear in mind that there is only a limited carrier transport system in place to deliver the stock. You may be able to arrange to collect the birds – a good option as you will see before you buy and will normally spend some fascinating time looking around the stock. Alternatively, the breeder may be able to arrange delivery or meet you somewhere with the birds – at a show is often a popular place for delivering birds.

Step 2: Contact the breeders
Once you have completed Step 1, you can begin to make contact with the reputable breeders. It is best to compile a shortlist of 3 or 4 breeders as it is possible that they may not have stock available to supply. Now is a good time to ask specific questions about the breed you have chosen and the strain (bloodline) that the breeder keeps, and clarify any queries you may have. A good reputable breeder should be very accommodating and helpful – try and remember that as the customer you are in the driving seat and not

under any obligation to purchase.

The process with commercial hybrids can be slightly easier, particularly if you can get hold of one of the magazines in which they advertise. Most of the varieties publish official selling agents with stock for sale – try to stick to these and you know you'll get the correct hybrid birds.

Step 3: Make the purchase
If everything is agreeable, you can purchase your new stock. In 1926, a prize-winning Buff Plymouth Rock cockerel was sold for £50. Fortunately, poultry prices have not increased in line with inflation and your stock should be much cheaper per bird. For chickens expect to pay at least £5-15 per bird but up to as much as £50 or £60 or even more for exceptional show stock. Ducks and geese can be in the same price range and frequently higher – they generally have a longer productive life than chickens. Turkeys are often scarcer so the price of stock can fluctuate and the average price is higher, nearer the £20-30 mark. Bear in mind that if you just want healthy birds and are not bothered about their 'quality', you can always obtain something cheaply. Laying hybrid varieties are much cheaper than pure-bred stock but bear in mind thay have little or no resale value. Point-of-lay females can be purchased for as little as £1 per bird but they often lack the attractiveness of the pure breeds. Remember also that the breeder should have something in your budget and you can negotiate the price.

Once purchased if you have any problems your first contact should be the vendor. Enjoy your birds!

How to Feed Correctly

Hens do not lay eggs for your breakfast of their own free will – in their natural state they would only lay the eggs they wished to sit upon, but man has bred the domestic hen to continue to lay eggs for a much longer period than in the natural state and to do this they **must be fed properly**. At most domestic waste should not account for more than a fifth of total feed.

Structure of the Chicken _____

To feed correctly it is necessary to know something of the internal structure of a chicken and, in particular, how they use their food.

The chicken's internal organs are in three divisions – respiratory, digestive and reproductive.

The respiratory organs are:

1 The nostrils through which air passes and where any solid particles are prevented from passing into the lungs;
2 The trachea, or windpipe, which begins at the glottis or slit at the back of the mouth;
3 The lungs, situated close up to the ribs between the shoulders.

First of the **digestive** organs is the crop, a bag at the bottom of the gullet (or throat) into which food is received immediately after being swallowed and before passing into the gizzard – a 'stomach' where the fowl pulps up the food for assimilation by the intestines.

In their daily wanderings chickens swallow a mixture of things – corn and seed, grass and other herbage, soft solids like bread and poultry meal, indigestibles like grit.

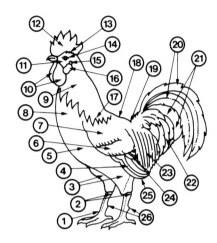

Fig. 28 Points of a fowl

1 Shank or leg	15 Ear
2 Hocks	16 Ear lobe (large and fleshy
3 Thighs	
4 Primaries	17 Cape
5 Point of heel-bone	18 Back
6 Wing coverts	19 Saddle
7 Wing – bow	20 Sickles
8 Breast	21 Tail (main feathers)
9 Neck hackle	22 Tail coverts
10 Wattles	23 Saddle hack
11 Face	24 Secondaries
12 Comb	25 Abdomen
13 Base of comb	26 Spurs
14 Cap	

Why Chickens Need Grit _____

The reason for supplying grit is to help chickens digest food – grit in their gizzard acts like teeth for the bird. Grain can be ground by normal muscular action of the gizzard, but not so efficiently, since grit greatly increases the number of grinding surfaces and consequently the food plant cells are broken down thus allowing the fullest action by the digestive juices.

Grit is also a means of supplying calcium, an essential part of poultry diet. Although this mineral is sometimes included in purchased balanced feeding stuffs it can also be given to the birds as soluble oyster shell or ground limestone.

Birds should have access to both the soluble and the insoluble grits (granite and flint usually) in separate containers. Insoluble grit can be retained in the gizzard for many months and adult requirements are under half a kilogram a year.

There is no predigestion process because a hen, unlike us, has no teeth and so all she eats passes into the crop where a softening process is started by a mixture of saliva and water.

The food then passes through the proventricle or stomach – a comparatively small organ in a fowl – and into the gizzard, where the food is ground up by strong muscular walls. From the gizzard the nutritives in food are, as in the human, acted upon by bile (a bitter fluid secreted by the liver and stored in the gall-bladder) and so into the blood.

How Eggs are Produced _____

The reproductive organs (testes) in the male fowl are high up in the abdomen, near the kidneys. In the female the egg organs are the ovary and the oviduct. There are, in a chick, two ovaries but only the lefthand one develops to maturity – and this is an unevenly-shaped bag, to which are attached the ova (or eggs).

The eggs develop one by one, become detached and slip into the oviduct – a long, twisted tube ending in the vent, or anus, of the bird through which the bird's droppings and eggs pass on leaving the body (Fig. 29).

The chicken's oviduct is in two parts. In the first portion the white (or albumen) is deposited around the yolk of the egg and in the second part of the oviduct the shell is made. To pass through the first portion of oviduct an egg takes between 3 and 5 hours, through the second 15 to 20 hours. The egg is then complete (Fig. 30) and ready to lay.

A Balanced Diet _____

Your birds need feedstuffs containing not only protein, fats and carbohydrates, but also vitamins and certain minerals. This is called a 'balanced' diet. A point to watch is that mineral supplements in purchased poultry feeds have a limited life – and the end date is stated on the contents specification label attached to the bags. When you open up the containers, check that this mineral life date has not expired; if it has, then ask your dealer to replace with fresher food. Otherwise you are wasting your money.

There is no particular merit in buying the individual components of a balanced diet because not only is it easy enough to purchase the **complete** food from a local farmer or agricultural merchant or town pet shop – but this way you will be certain that the 'mix' is correct.

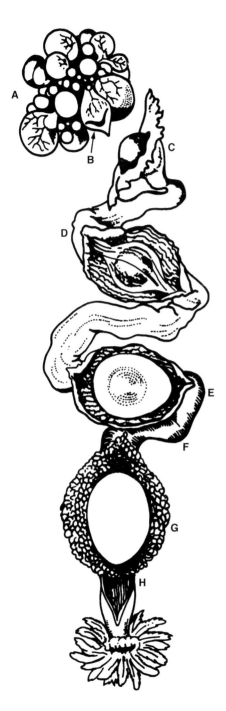

Fig. 29 (left) The development of an egg
A The ovary , showing yolks or 'ova' in different stages of development, held together like a cluster of grapes. As each yolk or ovum grows to its full size it drops off and passes through **B** the mouth ot the oviduct; **C** the open mouth receiving it. Immediately upon entering the oviduct it meets the spermatozoa and becomes fertilised. **D**, **E** and **G** show the egg in different stages during its passage to the outer world. It passes with a rotary motion, layers of albumen being twisted around it, first the shell-membrane is formed and afterwards the shell itself. It takes from 3 – 4 hours for the egg to pass down to point **D**, then 16 – 18 hours for the rest of the journey—so that often there are two or three eggs together in the oviduct. The point **F** indicates the last convolution of the passage, and the wall of the oviduct is thickest and strongest there—the shell having practically become hard; **G** shows it about to pass into the cloaca, and **H** the cloaca communicating with the outer world through the vent.

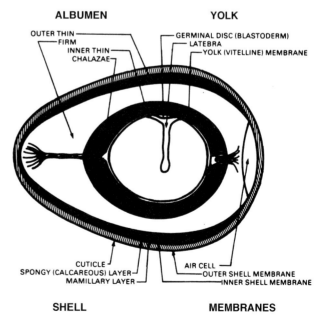

Fig. 30 The structure of an egg

Poultry need enough food to maintain their bodies and more to provide a constant supply of eggs. The choice of feedstuff is between mash, feed and grain.

Bigger, 'heavy' types of poultry eat more than smaller sized birds and all poultry eat more at one time, or one particular day, than at other times and for this reason it is difficult to give a precise measure of food required. However, for the average domestic unit 1 lb. (500 g) of pellets fed morning and late afternoon is quite sufficient for a flock of eight to ten birds.

If you use the 'hopper' system of feeding (see page 13) then, of course, the birds will help themselves. Good models of poultry feeders, and a homemade water receptacle, are shown in Figs. 31 and 32.

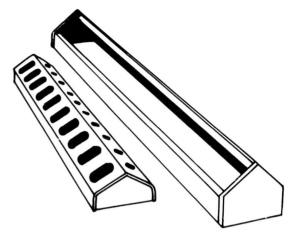

Fig. 31 Feeders

One System Only ⎯⎯⎯⎯⎯⎯⎯

'Mash' is the term applied to any balanced mixture of meal, while pellets refers to foods that have been ground and compressed into cylindrical form. Pellets are certainly very easy to feed and the size of these varies according to the age of the poultry. 'Crumbs' is food in a granular form.

Whichever system you adopt, use it regularly if you want the best results. Changes in the type and method of feeding only result in the birds being disturbed and that usually means fewer eggs.

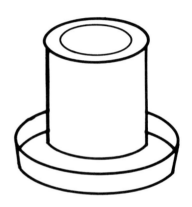

Fig. 32 Homemade watering can, made out of gallon oil can and pan

Pellets Easiest ⎯⎯⎯⎯⎯⎯⎯

Partly, the type of food you choose depends on the system of poultry keeping. For instance, if you are using the intensive system of housing then dry mash is probably the best because the process of eating keeps the birds more or less busy when they have nothing else to do! On the other hand, pellets are the easiest system of all since they are so easy to handle, are entirely clean and their cost is only slightly above that of dry meal.

Pellets are particularly popular with the domestic poultry keeper having a small outdoor poultry run because not only are the birds able to 'fill up' quickly but this very fact also leaves them maximum time for foraging in the run, the orchard, or whatever available land they have.

Pellets are also suitable for use in laying cages.

One obvious advantage of pellets is that you avoid the almost inevitable waste from dry mash feeding. A hopper full of pellets is as good a way of leaving your birds to fend for themselves for a few days and neither will pellets clog the hopper.

Wet Mash

The merit of wet mash feeding is that it allows the maximum use of vegetables and kitchen waste which can all be mixed up with the mash – but you must have ample trough space to allow all the birds to feed at once.

It is a mistake to think that adding water to a well balanced dry mash will necessarily add either to its nutritive value or its appeal to your poultry.

Different poultry foods absorb different amounts of water and you can only judge this at the time of actually mixing your mash. If you decide on this method of feeding, the rule is to make your mash moist but crumbly – not sloppy. If the mash breaks up easily when you pass a hand through it then that should be just about right.

Wet mash feeding, whatever its merits, is also a more laborious task.

Cooked Foods

Potatoes and household scraps must be thoroughly cooked before you feed it to poultry.

The main reason for this advice is to cut out the possibility of disease – but another advantage is that the birds will find your scraps more digestible when they are cooked.

The exception is other fresh vegetables and fruit which can be given raw or cooked.

The nutritional value of an egg is to some extent influenced by the diet, although the general protein and fat content remains fairly constant. The main point to watch is that whatever system of feeding you use the birds must have the right vitamin and mineral content. This is why in the long run it is safer to buy ready-mixed foods from the shop or local farmer, even if it is slightly more expensive than mixing your own feeding stuffs. Household scraps can be given to birds as a treat.

Loss of Appetite

It is important to keep an eye on the birds' daily habits.

Just like us, they sometimes lose their appetite – and there is usually a reason for this. An instance of this arises sometimes when the system of dry mash feeding is used. Unless the mash is stirred the birds may well find it stale and will not show much interest in adequate feeding. Never just put new food on top of old – not only will the birds not find it very appetising but the mash underneath can become mouldy and cause nutritional problems.

Unless you are using the 'self-service' hopper system (which means food is constantly available to the birds) it is best to feed adult stock only twice a day. Feed times should be as early as possible in the morning, as soon as the poultry house is opened up, and each late afternoon one hour before dusk – or in summer time about 6 pm. Hard corn is ideal for the evening meal whatever food programme you follow, but more so if the birds are on a mash diet.

Good Management

A common mistake among beginners is to assume that the more fowls they keep the higher their chances of plenty of fresh eggs. Even those who have been successful with, say, half a dozen hens, want to double the number in the belief that they can double the yield – and all this without increasing their poultry house accommodation.

Another common myth is that the birds will perform better if a cockerel runs with them. Not only can this be seen as a noise nuisance in built-up areas but, in fact, a male bird has no influence whatever upon egg production.

The only good reason for keeping a cockerel is for fertilising eggs when you want to hatch out your own replacement chicks – otherwise a cockerel in the hen yard creates a lot of noise and eats a lot of food!

Yet another mistaken notion is – more food equals more eggs. The result of this misguided kindness is that the birds soon become too fat to lay and develop liver complaints.

These mistakes are regrettable because a few fowls will pay you handsomely in eggs if your management is sensible. What, then, are the main ingredients of success for the amateur poultry keeper?

Success depends quite largely on whether you really **like** poultry keeping!

In other words, it is a matter of personal attention. Where fowls are kept in small houses cleanliness is of the greatest importance. Cleanliness, and being scrupulously careful not to leave traces of feeding stuffs around sheds, will also help to prevent rats and mice becoming a pest.

Stress has already been laid on the necessities of good housing, including the space to be allowed for each of your laying hens. Exercise is a good way of keeping hens occupied, so some type of covered-in run is essential. Otherwise the birds will become lazy in bad weather, staying in the poultry house to avoid the wet and to avoid the quagmire which an open run soon becomes in bad weather.

Water Supply

The importance of a good water supply cannot be exaggerated.

Poultry are naturally thirsty and will drink poor water if they get the chance, so always make sure that your birds have not only enough water but that it is **clean**.

Quality of Eggs

Foods (usually spicy) that tend to hasten production unduly may also lead to problems including eggs which are double yolked, soft shelled or mis-shapen.

Incorrect feeding can be the cause of very small eggs, one perfect egg being included in a second shell; or the production of the albumen (that is the white of the egg) and the shell but without any yolk.

Eggs with an unusually pale yolk are often the result of an anaemic condition in the hen brought about by under-feeding, close confinement, or an insufficient supply of green food and grain.

Winter Lighting

By artificially lengthening the hours of light during winter days, egg production can be considerably increased. For maximum winter production a pullet is said to need 14 hours of light a day – but one should remember that artificial lighting will not increase a bird's total **yearly** output of eggs; she simply lays more than she would normally do in the dark winter days, at the expense of her output from spring onwards.

A combination of morning and evening electric lights is the usual method, and by using a time switch the poultry keeper can avoid the chore of getting up early enough in the morning to switch on whilst it is still dark (and turning off each night). When the natural day lengthens to 14 hours again, the lights can be discontinued.

Lamps of 40 to 60 watt are powerful enough and one light fixture is adequate for the average sized domestic poultry house.

When electric lighting is first installed it may be necessary, for the first week or two, to catch and place the birds on the perches if they do not get on the roost of their own accord when it is time for 'lights out'. However, the birds soon get used to the idea – but do not forget they will expect (and need) extra rations if you put them on 'double shift' work!

Replacing Birds

There can be no doubt that the most economical plan is to clear out your old poultry every other year and then start again with fresh point-of-lay pullets (that is when they are about six months old), or even younger birds. The younger the new pullets, the cheaper – but you, rather than the breeder, will face the cost of feeding them until they are old enough to start laying.

The old birds to be dispensed with – or 'culled' from the flock as it is known – will make excellent boiling fowl or they can sometimes be sold live in your local market.

It certainly does not pay to keep hens after their second laying season; their feed costs may well increase and the birds lay fewer eggs. There is a temptation to the amateur – particularly parents – to keep hens too long because some of them tend to become children's pets!

Every 12 months, usually starting in early autumn, hens will moult. This is the term applied to the casting of their feathers and a rather sorry sight they look – so the time to sell your older birds is before they moult; if, however, they are destined for 'the pot' then looks will not bother you!

Coping with the Moult

A common cause of indifferent winter laying is that the hens have not been looked after properly during the moult. Improper care at this time makes the hens backward and unable to withstand winter conditions. By contrast, where hens are well looked after, properly fed and housed in warm and dry conditions, they quickly recover from the August– September moult.

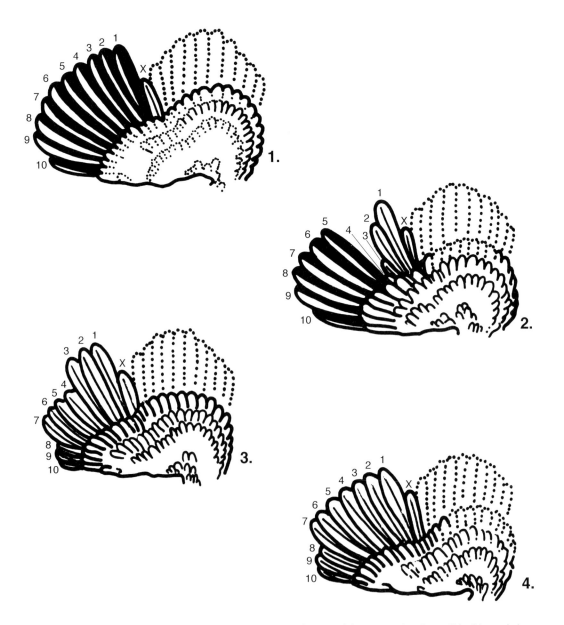

Fig. 33 Wings during different stages of moult. **1** shows the 10 old primary feathers (black), and the secondary feathers (broken outline), separated by the axial feather (x). **2** shows a slow moulter at six weeks of moult, with one fully grown primary and feathers 2, 3 and 4 developing at two-week intervals. In contrast **3**, a fast moulter, has all new feathers. Feathers 1 to 3 were dropped first, (now fully developed); feathers 4 to 7 were dropped next (now four weeks old); and feathers 8 to 10 were dropped last (now two weeks old). Two weeks later **4**, feathers 1 to 7 are fully grown.

A healthy yearling hen, one not too fat, takes no longer than about six weeks to change her feathers, whereas an old hen takes two and sometimes even three, months to complete the change. If the young hen, therefore, starts about the first week in August, she has finished by the middle of September, which gives her plenty of time to recover her form before the cold weather sets in. Such a hen should be ready to start laying again during the first half of November.

Some varieties of hens take much longer to pass through the moulting period than others – the laying or non-sitting breeds, such as the Leghorns, being generally at least a fortnight quicker than heavy breeds such as the Light Sussex or Rhode Island Red.

Restricted Feeding

During the first part of the moulting period food supply to the birds should be poor in quality and quantity to encourage the feathers to fall as quickly as possible. In fact, commercially, poultry keepers deprive the birds of food and water for up to 24 hours. However, as soon as the new feathers are being formed, make sure you **change back to concentrated food**

(see the chapter on How To Feed Correctly).

As moulting takes place during the summer, there is nothing very special to note regarding the housing of your birds. Just make sure they are warm at night and free from draughts.

Partial Moult

The beginner can often be troubled with an outbreak of what is called neck or partial moulting.

Partial moult usually happens during the early part of the year and may be a form of nature's protest against over forcing. For instance, the user of winter artificial lighting (see page 33) who has made his birds put in too much 'overtime', will probably get such a moult among his stock – the same thing happens to the novice who, having obtained good results, tries to force things still further by adding fish or other sources of high protein to his ration.

There is no doubt that the least likely bird to indulge in this partial change of plumage is the pullet who has been hatched in March or April and that has not been forced on unnaturally in any way, but just allowed to grow and develop in the open.

Some of the Problems

Feather Eating

Few of the troubles that beset the poultry keeper are more annoying than feather eating. It is not a disease, merely a bad habit – but it is most difficult to get rid of and can often lead to the deaths of the birds attacked.

Often one old hen will start it and she teaches the trick to all her colleagues in the flock. The necks and rumps of every bird soon become denuded of feathers and they present a very sorry sight.

The trouble usually starts in confined runs, presumably because the birds are idle. However, it is also partly a craving for something not supplied in the birds' food and more often than not, this is found to be green food.

One of the best remedies, obtainable from chemists or farmers, is a very strong solution of quassia, a bitter substance sometimes used as a tonic in medicine, which can be dabbed onto the birds' feathers without harm. Another cure for it is to use proprietary brands of anti-pecking powder. A good plan is to hang cabbages up in the poultry run just above the birds' heads so that they have to jump up in order to peck them. Diversion of this sort will clear the blood and provide scratching exercise and will do more than anything else to stop the nuisance.

Egg Eating

Another bad habit is egg eating – often acquired in the first instance as a result of birds producing eggs without shells or dropping an egg from the perch when roosting. In either case, the hen or hens, naturally enough, investigate the character of the contents and, having once tasted an egg, they will do it again!

If you always allow your fowls free access to a good supply of broken oyster shell and fresh green food, this will largely prevent egg eating ever starting. This is another instance where poultry kept with an adequate run are better than those in too confined a space – the theory being that a busy hen seldom makes a nuisance of herself.

Egg Binding

This arises principally in two ways – either the oviduct is too small to allow passage of the egg or the egg has become broken and will not therefore slip out properly.

The oviduct of a pullet when she first begins to lay is a narrow passage and the first few eggs will not find their way through without causing the bird a little pain and difficulty. Most cases of egg binding can be relieved by holding the hen for a little time with her vent exposed to the steam from boiling water – this softens the fat and the pelvic bones, and if the bird is then given some olive oil and placed in a comfortable strawed box she will usually expel the egg within a couple of hours.

If you have not kept poultry before, you may be rather worried when you find your first eggs to be of an odd, long and rather narrow shape and possibly streaked with blood. There is, in fact, no need to worry and the reasons are obvious: the resistance of the narrow passage causes the long shaped egg and the rupture of small vessels as it forces its way through accounts for the blood streaks.

Prolapse

This condition, sometimes termed 'down-behind', is fairly common and is one which causes a proportion of the hen's organs to protrude. It is caused by straining and it most often happens to hens that are very fat or have been overlaying.

The only thing that can be done is to clean and then smear the part with a lubricating jelly and carefully push it back.

Having done this, put the hen away by herself for a week or more, only giving a moderate amount of food in order to check production of eggs for a time. If protrusion of the intestines recurs then wash or sponge it each time it appears and gently push it back again. Perseverance usually results in a cure.

The Common Cold

This is caused by a virus, quickly spread by overcrowding the birds or in houses with poor ventilation. Sometimes the birds are prone to colds simply through bad feeding or nostrils.

Egg production falls badly, the poultry seem to lose their appetite, and they sneeze frequently with mucous running from their eyes. Hens do not generally die from this complaint and it usually passes away in a few weeks.

If the colds are only slight, a little sulphate of iron in the drinking water helps – 30 gms (about 1 oz) dissolved in ½ litre of water (about 1 pint) and from this solution use two tablespoonful in each gallon of drinking water.

For bad cases of colds in fowls, the affected birds should be isolated and given the drug Aureomycin, added to drinking water. The drug is obtainable through veterinary sources only.

Roup

If neglected, the common cold soon develops into roup. In 'wet' roup there is an offensive discharge from the breathing tubes but the complaint – although very contagious – can be cured by using pure sulphate of copper. Dissolve 30 gms (roughly 1 oz) in about ¼ litre of water (½ pint) and use the fowls' drinking water at a rate of two teaspoonful to each ½ litre (1 pint) of water. If many birds are affected, isolation is useless and the above remedy should be doubled in strength and given to the entire flock.

'Dry' roup is a similar condition, but with comparatively little discharge.

Cramp

This is a common ailment of growing stock, arising from imperfect circulation or through damp and cold conditions underfoot. It affects the legs, causing the bird to squat down helplessly, and the hen's toes are often contracted.

The remedy is a change to better conditions – long straw in a dry pen is excellent – and regular rubbing of the hen's legs with a penetrating liniment or even turpentine.

Liver Disease

The cause of this disease, with a heavy mortality rate, is a tuberculosis bacillus which attacks the liver and neck glands in poultry (it is not the same bacillus which causes tuberculosis in man and in cattle).

Lameness in one leg is a preliminary sign and later on a thinning of the flesh on one, or both sides, of the breast-bone (hence the disease being called 'going light').

A mixture of Glauber and Epsom salts is sometimes given, or used as a preventive, but humanely dispatching and **burning** of the carcasses is the only sure way of ridding the poultry unit of this disease.

Crop Bound

One of the commonest of all poultry complaints is congestion of the crop.

For some reason or another the food in the hen's crop cannot be persuaded to pass through and consequently becomes unwholesome with fermentation occurring. The hen will be seen to have a full crop even before the morning feed.

The main causes are either an obstruction (sometimes a twisted ball of long grass), indigestion, or general debility. The best cure is to give the hen a drink of warm water to distend the crop, which should then be softened by rubbing gently with one's hand. Hold the bird

with its head downwards, squeeze her crop and often the liquid will run out. Finish the treatment by letting the hen drink freely, preferably warm water containing a little Epsom salts and bicarbonate of soda (one teaspoonful is enough). Put the hen in a dry pen for 24 hours and restrict feed.

Pests and other Enemies

In previous sections on housing and poultry management, stress has been laid on the need for cleanliness. One of the main reasons for this is to avoid trouble from pests and various insects, the most common of these being a parasite called Red Mite (see Fig. 34) and the Hen Flea (Fig. 35).

Red Mite feed on the birds at night and are so frequently overlooked until their damage is severe. During the day the mites hide in crevices, perch sockets and nest boxes – if you suspect or see signs of infection you must thoroughly clean and disinfect the entire poultry house. (Incidentally, the easiest way of finding out whether there are Red Mite is to examine your poultry house by torchlight at night – the presence of Red Mite is also shown up by 'salt and pepper' markings on the perches and elsewhere.) The Hen Flea lives in the underfluff of a bird's feather and feeds on the feather matter. Yellowish in colour, they can be seen with the naked eye when the feathers are lifted.

When you are cleaning up the poultry house it is quite effective if you spray with either paraffin or creosote as a solution for this trouble. Louse powder is available from many agricultural merchants or pet stores. Another useful point to remember is to avoid bringing in parasite infection when you buy second-

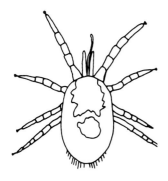

Fig. 34 Adult female Red mite (magnified 45 times)

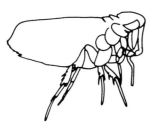

Fig. 35 Hen flea (Pulex avium). Actual size about 3mm

hand equipment – always clean it thoroughly before use.

Apart from the fox, the amateur is most likely to be troubled, particularly if he lives in a town, either by cats or rats.

As far as cats are concerned, it is best to make sure your stock is properly protected with the use of adequate wire netting. There is, in fact, not much else you can do.

Rat Proof

Rats are, however, another matter. Again, use small mesh wire netting plus consistent poisoning whenever rats are seen to be about.

Gardens previously free from rats will often attract the pest when poultry are kept – no doubt brought in by the smell of good food. It is important to keep your feeding stuffs in secure rat-proof tins (a new dustbin is excellent for the job).

Rearing Chicks

Many poultry keepers decide they would like to breed from their flock and baby chicks can be particularly popular with children.

If this is the case, and none of your well-managed hens has gone broody (the term given to a hen who wishes to sit and, with or without eggs under her, stays put in a nest box), a friend might well lend you a broody bird under which you could place 12 to 15 fertile eggs. It is an intriguing side to poultry keeping – but it demands under-standing and considerable care. The housing needs of a broody hen and her chicks are explained in the set of drawings shown in Figs. 36 to 43.

To take a broody hen from the nest of her choice and place her down upon eggs shut up in a box you have made yourself is, from the bird's point of view, not very appealing.

Try to introduce the broody bird gently to your selected nest site, preferably in the evening, so that by the following morning she may be a little more reconciled to her artificial quarters.

It is a good idea to place a few china or plastic eggs in the nest to begin with and, after the sitting hen has once been out to feed and has returned to settle down again on the eggs, substitute the real eggs for hatching under the bird at night.

The Broody

The first thing to remember if you are going to sit a broody hen is that you must make some concession to the bird's natural instincts.

Fig. 36 When a layer is still on the nest at dusk it can be assumed that she is broody

If the broody hen is not wanted for chick rearing she is placed in a coop with slatted floor—the discomfort puts the bird off further sitting.

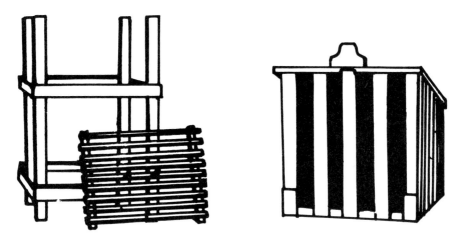

Fig. 37 Handy back garden coop. As can be seen (together with Fig. 39) the maximum use can be made from a coop by making it go with a stand and slatted floor

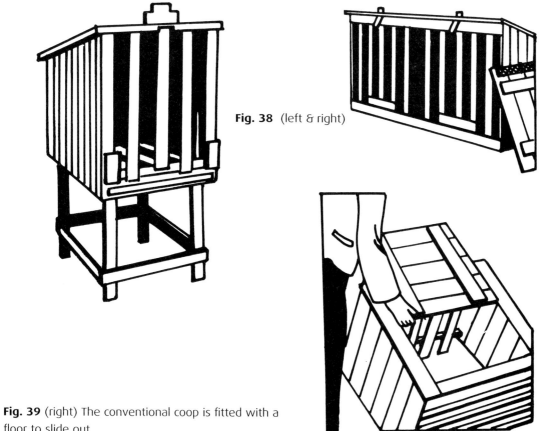

Fig. 38 (left & right)

Fig. 39 (right) The conventional coop is fitted with a floor to slide out

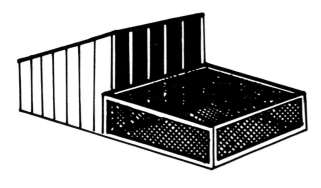

Fig. 40 For mother hen with her chicks

Fig. 41 (right) The receptacles on the top of the run are for grit and water. For a start it is necessary to feed the chicks in the coop above where the hen will teach them to eat

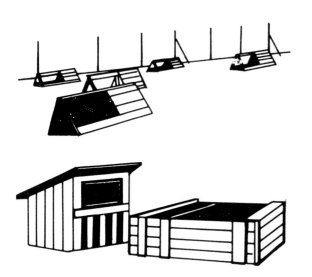

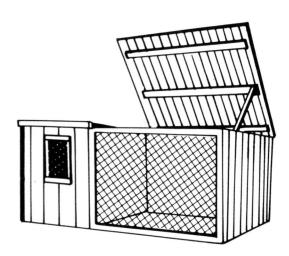

Fig. 42 A fold-type unit used for hens with chicks on a small poultry farm. The outfit above shows a further variation in style of coop

Fig. 43 A double coop is very useful for a hen and chicks. The roof opens up to permit feeding and watering

Gentle Handling

Good management of sitting hens requires gentle handling throughout the process of incubation. Each day give the hen enough time for feeding, exercise and scratching about in a dust bath. The hen should be free, and off the nest, for about a quarter of an hour each day.

If the weather is very bad, give your hen some scratching material in a shed and scatter the corn in there to induce her to take enough exercise – and here comes a warning: on no account let your hen re-enter the nest box until she has produced some droppings, otherwise she will almost certainly foul her nest and the sitting eggs. Should she by chance do so, or soil her feathers by means of a broken egg, then you must clean up the bird.

Start of Incubation

When incubation begins the hen often endeavours to sit tight on the nest, ignoring the necessity for food and exercise. When this happens you should lift the hen gently from her eggs and place her down outside the nest box and within sight of the food and water.

When a hen, whose previous behaviour has been normal, shows a strong disinclination to leave the nest within a day of the due date for hatching, then do not disturb her. The hen's action at this time is directed by her natural instinct regarding the immediate requirements of the nearly due chickens within the shells.

Completion of the development of the embryo varies a little but normally the perfected chick should be ready to break the enclosing shell sometime during the 21st day of incubation. As soon as shell chipping has begun then feed and water the hen without taking her off the nest; any chilling of the eggs at this time is harmful, sometimes even fatal.

Birth of the Chicks

At actual hatching time it is best to 'leave well alone' – like any other mother, the hen knows well enough what to do.

Usually, from the start of the chipping it will take between six and 10 hours for the chick to emerge completely from the shell. All that you need do is to remove the empty egg shells by placing your hand beneath the hen during the hatching process.

If there should be undue delay in the chick emerging, all that can be done safely consists of the further breaking of an already chipped shell and the gentle tearing of the shell membrane if this is unusually dry or tough. As a general rule, however, do not interfere.

Transferring to Coop

Before they get their first meal (see page 45 for guidance on feeding chicks) after incubation, chicks and mother should be transferred to a coop. Let the hen examine the coop and settle down in a brooding attitude before you let her have all the chicks. At this stage dust her with insect powder to free her from pest insects.

When a hen, after sitting tight for two or three weeks, has finished hatching her brood she deserves a good feed of maize and wheat before taking up again her maternal vigil.

Artificial Rearing

The Incubator

An alternative to using your own broody hen is to buy fertile eggs and use a small incubator. There are many of these sold by the poultry appliance makers and, provided you follow the maker's instructions and the rules below, you should be successful:

- Use only well-shaped, good sized eggs less than a week old, marking the date on them when placed in the incubator. Do not load the incubator with too many eggs.
- Situate the incubator free from draughts and from sunshine and heat it running at about 40°C.
- Throughout incubation keep the water tray in the incubator topped up so that the eggs have adequate moisture – and turn the eggs, in opposite directions, three or four times a day.

At seven and 14 days it is possible to check for fertility, removing any infertile eggs which will be 'clear' if held to the light. As soon as the chicks begin to chip the egg shells at, or about, the 19th day, leave the incubator alone. On the 21st morning, inspect the interior and see that all is well with the hatched chicks – but do not remove or assist chicks from the shell. For 24 hours leave the chicks undisturbed, after which they can be removed in a warm, protected basket to the brooder for rearing.

When the chicks are hatched they can either be transferred to a brooder (see below) or put under a hen which has been sitting for three weeks or so and has some chicks of her own. If you try this method of rearing you must place the new chicks gently under the hen whilst she is on the nest, but the incubator-hatched chicks must be of the same colour as the hen's own chicks, otherwise the hen will probably kill the 'foreign' chickens. Poultry have a keen sense of colour, even if they cannot count!

The Brooder

This is an appliance for the artificial rearing of chicks hatched in an incubator.

A brooder is made with a metal or wooden floor and sides, with only one way out for the chicks. Although there are plenty of good brooders on the market the handyman can easily make his own provided he remembers to have three parts in the brooder – one for sleeping, another for feeding and exercise, and a third as an outer run on grass, but this must be covered and have a wire netting front to let the light in.

In winter time your chicks will remain in a brooder until they are at least six weeks old. The brooder can be heated either by an infra-red lamp (see Figs. 44 and 45) which is cheap and effective to operate, by an electric heating

Fig. 44 An infra-red brooder

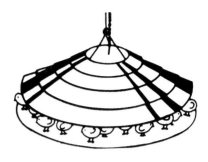

Fig. 45 A hover-type brooder

element or by a domestic light bulb. Keep the heat in the brooder around 35°C, reducing this two or three degrees each week. At six to eight weeks old your chicks may manage without artificial heat, providing they are sufficiently feathered up.

Feeding New Chicks

For the first ten or 14 days chicks are fed on dry chick crumbs which is the normal powdery mash processed into fragments. This is available from your pet shop or farmer – or, if you have a grinder, you could make your own from the following seeds: canary seed (3 parts), millet seed (2 parts), groats (also 2 parts) and one part each of hempseed and finely cracked peas. After about 10 days, add an equal portion of finely cracked wheat. A week later still, add a little small maize and broken chicken rice.

For either artificially reared chicks, or those under a hen, 'little and often' is sound feeding

advice – at least every three or four hours. At all times leave the birds an adequate fresh water supply.

When your chicks are about a month old they should be given **alternate** meals of soft and hard food (such as broken corn), but feed the corn later in the day rather than the morning.

Keep Them Growing

You must, if the chicks are to grow, keep them 'moving' throughout their first weeks and to do this means feeding them properly, keeping them free from colds and disease and providing the young stock with sufficient exercise.

Until they are a month old they should be fed five or six times a day; until they are three months old, four times a day; and from then until they are adult birds, three times.

Chicks look so frail but are, in fact, surprisingly strong. Provided they are not in cold or damp conditions they will grow quickly.

Handling Poultry

Poultry should never be handled carelessly or roughly. The easiest way to catch and pick up hens is shown in Figs. 46 and 47.

Carrying live birds by their legs or wings can easily result in damage, and no more than two adult birds should be carried at one time (despite the rough handling of several birds at a time as one frequently sees in the markets). Careful and correct carrying is shown in Fig. 48.

When a bird has been caught, the best method for inspecting your hen is to pass your hand under the bird's breast, from the front, and grip each thigh between two fingers. Next, raise the bird and tuck it away beneath the arm, lightly but firmly pressing the wings between your elbow and body – the bird's head thus pointing backwards (see Fig. 49). A broody hen will be seen to have lost most of the breast feathers (Fig. 50).

Taking a Look

The domestic poultry keeper should regularly examine his stock, if not for replacement purposes then certainly to see whether or not they are doing well. The best time to do this is

Fig. 46 To catch a particular hen, try to separate the bird you want from the others, corner her and close in

at dusk when they have just settled down on the perches – first you can note the state of their crops, whether they are full or otherwise, and from this deduce whether or not you are giving the birds enough food. Before you return the birds to their perches, also examine them for lice and mites.

A bird in good form should be solid to the feel without undue heaviness or flabbiness.

Fig. 47 The correct method of picking up a bird

Fig. 48 For carrying, the bird, held in the manner above, is tucked beneath the arm. The rear should be higher than the head

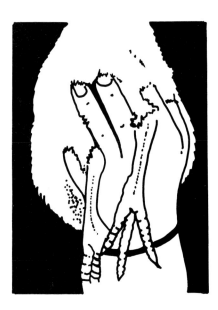

Fig. 49 The hand is slipped beneath the bird and the middle fingers between the legs as shown

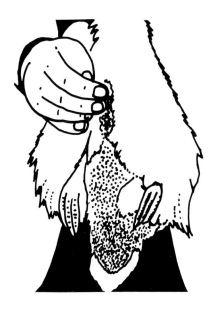

Fig. 50 A broody hen shows loss of feathers from the breast

Poultry for Table

Since, as already pointed out, it does not pay to keep hens after their second laying season, eating these old hens is the best bet – and you will already have had the benefit of a plentiful supply of eggs. There is another point about eating one's own poultry – even an old hen simmered for two or three hours and then browned in the oven is worth far more on one's own family table than the price you would get for such a hen.

If you decide to fatten up a few birds, then confine them as much as possible in the poultry house, otherwise the birds will run off the weight they gain. It is also helpful to cover the windows and provide semi-darkness between meals.

For fattening up purposes, whether it is an old hen or cockerels reared specially for the table, meals should preferably be of the wet mash type – plus waste milk if ever you get it – and mixed corn. Powdered milk is also a great help.

How to Pluck

Once a bird has been humanely and correctly slaughtered, plucking is easier before a bird becomes cold, since feathers come out more easily whilst the flesh is warm.

If for some reason the bird cannot be plucked at once, then it is best to leave it until quite cold – do not attempt to pluck poultry

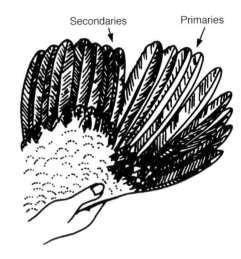

Fig. 51

in a half cold state as the skin will be torn and the bird spoiled.

The best way to pluck a hen is to sit on a low chair holding the bird by the legs and wings with the head dangling downwards. The feathers must be plucked the **reverse** way from that in which they lie on the body.

Start on the back first, taking several feathers between your thumb and first finger of the right hand – then give a sharp pull backwards. Part of the art is to pull the feathers **quickly** to avoid tearing the skin.

After you have plucked the back of the bird, turn her over and pull the feathers from the breast and under part. Pluck the bird's neck up to within a few inches of the head, always leaving the feathers on the top part of the neck. Next the legs should be plucked, stripping the feathers off down close to the shanks; wings are next (see Fig. 51) and these take a little longer to complete owing to the larger feathers or flights which have to be pulled out two or three at a time. The tail feathers come last and these should be pulled out one at a time or the flesh may be torn.

Preparing for Oven

With the bird plucked and the head removed from the neck at the point of dislocation, lay it on the work surface on its back and take a grip between finger and thumb of the flesh just below the breastbone. With a sharp knife cut horizontally into the flesh and layer of fat to a depth of about 1 inch (25 mm), taking care not to burst the gut.

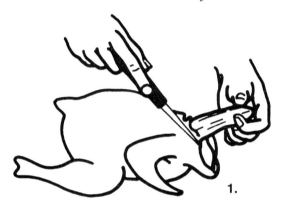

Fig. 52 The neck is cut off as close to the shoulders as possible

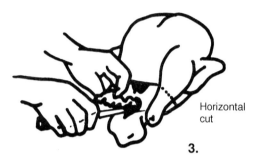

Fig. 54 The vent is loosened by cutting around it—be careful not to cut into the intestine. The entrails are removed through a short, horizontal cut about 5cm below the cut made around the vent

Fig. 53 The oil sac on the back near the tail should be cut out, as it sometimes gives a peculiar flavour to the meat. Remove it with a wedge shaped cut

Fig. 55 A well-trussed bird is a pleasing sight. In the methd shown here the legs are placed under the strip of skin between the vent opening and the cut from which the intestines were removed

You can then put your hand into the carcass and draw out the entrails. From what you remove in this piece of bird surgery, the heart, liver, outer case of the gizzard (that is a second stomach where the bird grinds its food) and the remainder of the neck are known as the giblets – very nice for simmering down into a broth.

When you are drawing a bird try not to break or tear any of the organs but, should this happen, wipe out the mess with a damp cloth or paper towels – it is unwise to wet the carcass by washing unless the bird is being cooked immediately (Figs. 52 to 55).

The job is complete when you have pulled off the remainder of the neck, folded the skin over the resulting hole, and trussed the bird by tying the 'drumsticks' to the 'parson's nose'. Do this in a tidy manner and you will be justifiably proud of your art.

The home quick freezer is particularly useful for storing oven-ready poultry, either whole or in pieces. The birds must, of course, first be 'dressed' (i.e., internal organs removed as described above) and placed in moisture-resistant wrappers before freezing.

Chicken should not be stuffed before freezing as this limits the storage life of the bird. (A stuffed chicken should be eaten within a month.) Store the giblets, wrapped separately, beside the bird.

Joints of chicken take up less freezer space than whole birds. To joint a fowl for the freezer, cut it in half through the breast bone and back

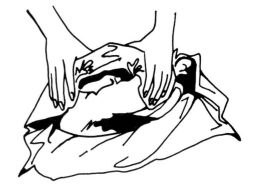

Fig. 56 Wrapping a chicken

bone – then cut each half into two or three pieces. Pack on an aluminium or fibre food tray and, finally, wrap with foil or polythene (see Fig. 56).

The quick freeze process works on the principle that the product is frozen so rapidly that no internal changes – for example, loss of moisture – can take place. The freezing is done rapidly at temperatures ranging from about –18°C to –34°C with the result that the natural quality, flavour and appearance of the birds are preserved.

Uses of Poultry Manure

Poultry manure is extremely useful for the garden and a very useful by-product of poultry keeping. A sign of this is that lawns on which poultry have been allowed to roam can become very lush and green!

Poultry manure is far richer in sulphate of ammonia, super phosphate and potash salts than farmyard manure. Its richness is due to the large amount of plant food elements that pass quickly through the fowl, and to its content of semi-solid urine, the white part of the droppings, with its nitrogen content.

As it is rapidly available, and much of the value can be washed away by rain, poultry manure is best applied in the spring. Use it in the vegetable plot and for your flowers but it is not recommended for apples and pears, although it is certainly most useful for soft fruit growing.

Good for Tomatoes

The standard dressing of poultry manure for the vegetable garden and the flower borders is about 4 oz (90 g) to the square yard (metre) forked in during February and March – preferably when you have limed the garden the previous Autumn. Never mix lime and poultry manure, or dig them in within three months of each other, or both will be wasted.

During the Summer you can use your poultry manure as a quick acting tonic. It can also be used with tomatoes, potatoes and onions, but in these cases it requires a 'balancer' dressing of potash.

Better Compost

Poultry manure also helps you to make more and better compost.

If swift heating of compost is to be secured there must be a great increase of bacteria in a short time and these require readily available nitrogen and phosphorus. This is where your poultry manure comes in.

One good way to acquire a supply of this valuable material is to build a heap consisting of a base of compost, followed by an inch (20 to 30 mm) of poultry manure, then more vegetable waste, followed by a layer of 2 inches (50 mm) of soil (plus a sprinkling of lime), more compost material and then back to your poultry manure.

Choosing the Right Breed – Chickens

Part of the pleasure of keeping chickens is to know something about the various breeds and how to distinguish them – and of course making your own particular choice. Breeds are very distinctive, not only in colour and shape but also in features like the feather markings and combs (see Figs. 57 and 58).

There are hundreds of different pure breeds and varieties of chickens presenting a difficult choice for the aspiring poultry keeper. Each of these breeds has distinct attributes and character, and is classified accordingly. This can also be based on a breed's historical origins, original purpose, popularity, or size.

Two sizes of chickens exist – 'large fowl' and 'bantam.' Both sizes can be found in many breeds, the bantam version having been created as a miniature of the large. 'True bantams', are those with no large counterpart and the breeds under this heading are usually for ornamental purposes. Large fowl require more room than bantams and consume more food but are generally more docile and obviously offer a larger carcass should you require birds for the table. Some bantams lay very well, although the egg is slightly smaller.

In fowl, another important distinction is that made between 'hard' and 'soft' feather breeds. Generally speaking, the 'hard' feather breeds are the 'game' varieties, whose historical origins lie in the outlawed pursuit of cockfighting. Having been developed over generations for exhibition purposes, they would be most unsuitable for this now. As the term suggests, they also have tighter feathering. The 'soft' feather breeds are those remaining.

The final classification amongst the soft feather varieties is into 'heavy' or 'light' types. The former are typically derived from breeds

Fig. 57 (left) Nine types of feather marking
1 Self; **2** Tipping; **3** Spangling; **4** Barring; **5** Striping; **6** Pencilling; **7** Peppering or Smut; **8** Single lacing; **9** Double lacing

Pea   Leaf   Horn

Rose   Strawberry   Single

Fig. 58 Types of comb

or sizes within a breed) can be very difficult to obtain as their numbers have diminished. Having provided a foundation for commercial poultry production, many breeds faced extinction in the post-war period as a result of hybridisation. Many are now in the hands of a limited number of enthusiasts.

A selection of breeds is outlined below. As with any livestock, once you have made your choice it is vital to purchase stock from reputable breeders who should provide you with quality well-bred birds that have been cared for properly.

that were originally bred for the table or dual-purpose (meaning they were good layers as well). The latter were derived from the breeds specifically for egg production and because of that rarely seem to go 'broody'.

Many of the once-popular breeds (or varieties

Dual-purpose breeds – for eggs and the table

The **Old English Game** (Fig. 59) is a breed that has historically been used for cockfighting. Available in large fowl and bantam these origins fail to credit the breed for its many

Fig. 59 The Old English Game bantam

53

qualities: grace, activeness, self-sufficiency, and colour. The bantam is the most popular bantam of all in Great Britain and probably the most popular pure breed bantam in the world. The breed is particularly hardy and active, and surprisingly docile in nature. The adult males need to have combs surgically removed for showing but, that aside, it makes a good breed for the farmyard or to add colour to a garden and will produce good numbers of eggs.

As the name suggests the **Rhode Island Red** (Fig. 60) was first developed in Rhode Island State, USA, in the 1830s. Eggs from the breed were sent to the UK in 1903, and the American Standard established in 1904. Available in large and bantam and often affectionately termed, 'Rhodies', these fowls have a broad, deep, brick-shaped body, flat back and medium sized tail with prominent eyes and yellow legs. The male plumage is glossy, rich, lustrous and dark red. Rhode Island Reds are active birds, which enjoy scratching about, particularly on

grass. Classed as a dual-purpose heavy breed, they lay good numbers of tinted eggs.

The **Sussex** (Fig. 61) is a very well-known British heavy breed derived from the original Old Sussex fowls, bred for their meat and eggs in Victorian times. The formation of the 1903 Sussex Breed Club led to further development in colours and varieties, many with beautiful feather patterns. Sussex are graceful, possessing a long, broad, flat back, tail at an angle of 45 degrees, fine neat head and a medium sized single comb. The eyes of darker colours are red, the lighter ones, orange, but all colours should have red earlobes and white legs and feet. The breed comes in large and bantam sizes, with the Light Sussex – predominantly white with a black-striped neck, wings, and tail – being by far the most popular. This is another layer of tinted eggs.

The **Plymouth Rock** is traditionally classified as a dual or general purpose heavy breed and is a bird of graceful curves with a large compact

Fig. 60 The Rhode Island Red

Fig. 61 The Light Sussex

Fig. 62 The Plymouth Rock, various colours

body, broad back and breast, medium upright single comb, yellow legs and rich bay eyes. Large and bantam versions are available, in various colours, but by far the most popular are the Buff (a pale orange) and Barred (Fig. 62) which are almost unique in their colour and markings. Large White Plymouth Rocks are currently used as the female line in 95% of the world's meat chicken breeding stocks. Quick maturing, the breed is a very good layer of tinted eggs and is very hardy.

The **Orpington** (Fig. 63) was named after the home town in Kent of William Cook who created the original utility Black variety in 1866. When superseded by a large feathery

Fig. 63 A Champion large fowl Black Orpington male – the breed is often described as being 'regal', its abundant feathering adding to the huge appearance.

exhibition bird, Cook responded by producing the Buff. Now there are other colours. One of the 'heavier' heavy breeds, Orpingtons have a deep broad body, the back appearing short with a somewhat concave shape. The head is neat with a single comb. Dark colours have dark eyes and legs, paler colours have red eyes and white legs. Chicks can take longer to feather than some other breeds. Orpingtons regularly take top show awards.

Most famous for its deep brown eggs, the **Marans** originated in France and were introduced in England in 1929. The body is of medium length with good width. Marans have high tails, complementing a neat head with a single comb and prominent eye. All colours have orangey-red eyes, with red earlobes and white legs. They mature quickly for a heavy breed, reaching 6-7lbs in six months. Day-old males have a white spot on the top of the head, females a darker one which makes sexing chicks fairly easy. Both bantam and large fowl are available.

Another of the 'heavier' heavy breeds, the **Wyandotte** (Fig. 64) was developed in North America from many other breeds. Its name is derived from the American Indian tribe, 'Wy-an-dot'. The first standardised colour was the very attractive Silver Laced in 1883, which arrived in England soon after this date. Subsequent crossbreeding created wide variations in colour and plumage, the most popular being laced and pencilled varieties. Available in large and bantam sizes the Wyandotte is curvy, with broad back, upright tail and short, broad, rose-combed head and neck. Its clean legs are yellow and its eyes bright bay. The exhibition whites regularly take top prizes and some utility strains still exist.

Fig. 64 The White Wyandotte

The **Silkie** (Fig. 65) deserves inclusion in this category for its almost unique qualities. The breed is best known for two endearing qualities – its soft, silky, fluffy feathering, and its persistent maternal instinct which makes it an excellent broody. Another unusual trait is its very dark meat and skin colour – the meat has often been considered a good substitute for pheasant meat. A relatively small large fowl, a tiny bantam has been recently created and developed good support. The Silkie has a stylish, compact, and lively demeanour and the mulberry head features, crest, five toes, and feathered legs add to its attractiveness. The Silkie has a gentle disposition, and is not flighty. They are undemanding in their requirements, but because of their type of feathering, they should always have dry and warm accommodation available to them, particularly when there's rain about.

Fig. 65 The Silkie

The light breeds – if eggs are the most important factor! ───────

The **Leghorn** (Fig. 66) is a famous light breed and was exported to many countries of the world from the Italian port of Leghorn. The Leghorn was, and still is, a prolific egg layer and the White Leghorn has figured prominently in the modern-day establishment of high egg-producing commercial hybrids. There are many colours standardised in both large fowl and bantam, though the Whites and Blacks are the most popular. Females have a folded single comb and males look grand with a large red comb and white ear lobes. The Leghorn is a striking, competitive breed for anyone, whether your aim is to win 'Best in Show' or to keep the household well supplied with white shelled eggs.

The **Araucana** (Fig. 67) arrived in Britain from South America in the 1920s and the breed is noted for its unusual 'blue' shelled eggs. The Lavender is the most popular colour, although there are many others - all the recognised

Fig. 66 The Leghorn

Fig. 67 The Aracuana

'game' colours are in the standard. The other distinguishing feature is its facial muffing and medium sized crest, together with a strong orange eye and curved beak giving an almost 'eagle like' expression. Many people keep Araucanas just for their blue eggs, especially the egg exhibitors. The Araucana is an attractive bird to keep in the garden and lays well most of the year.

The **Minorca** (Fig. 68) can be traced back in Britain to 1780 but its origins lie in Spain, perhaps originally as the 'Castillian'. By selective breeding, the head features of the Minorca became famous during the twentieth century, with the white almond shaped lobes particularly striking. Blacks are the predominant colour in both large and bantam, although Blues and Whites are sometimes available, along with a rose-combed version. They are noted egg producers and although classified as a 'light' breed, the weight of the birds can be quite surprising. The Minorca is a graceful bird with an excellent temperament and thrives on human contact.

Fig. 68 The Minorca

The **Welsummer** was imported into the UK from Holland in the 1920s, at a time when dark brown coloured eggs were much in demand. The breed is hardy and thrives under free range conditions producing good numbers of its dark brown, 'flowerpot' coloured eggs. Although classified as a 'light' breed and usually very active, their bodies are fairly large and the birds quite docile. Most people consider the colouring very attractive and reminiscent of a traditional 'farmyard' bird. Both large fowl and bantam versions are standardised, and there is also an attractive silver duckwing version.

True bantams – little gems, ideal where space is limited

The tiny **Dutch** (Fig. 69) originates in Holland, first appeared in Britain in the late 1960s, and has since gone from strength to strength. Numerous attractive colour varieties are available. Dutch bantams are popular both as exhibition birds and pets, with their upright and jaunty appearance and active nature making them very appealing. Dutch reproduce very well, and the females will sit their own eggs. They are ideal for young people and their size makes them easy to handle and popular where space is limited.

The **Pekin** (Fig. 70) is a charming breed with profuse plumage, good temperament, and must look as globular as possible from every angle, together with forward 'tilt'. The breed also has feathered feet. It was introduced to Britain from Pekin, China, in about 1860 following the Anglo-French expedition. The Pekin is a good breed for children and beginners, for pleasure or exhibition. For breeding, some clipping of vent and foot feathering may

Fig. 69 Two proud young poultry keepers showing off their favourite birds. On the left is a colourful Dutch bantam male, on the right a Sikie bantam female with unique 'fluffy' feathering. Both breeds are very good for children.

Fig. 70 An outstanding Pekin female of the mottled variety displaying typical breed characteristics of forward tilt and globular appearance. Another good breed to choose for children or the less mobile as they are easy to handle and very docile.

be necessary and although they are active little birds they do not do well in muddy conditions due to their foot feathering.

The **Sebright** (Fig 71) is one of the oldest British breeds, having been created by the baronet, Sir John Sebright well over 150 years ago. There are two varieties: the Golds and the Silvers. Both are very striking birds to look at, with their distinct feather-edge lacing. They are not particularly robust, and can be difficult to reproduce. The males are 'hen feathered', having none of the long sickle feathers belonging to males of other breeds.

Fig. 71 The Sebright

The **Rosecomb** is another of the oldest British breeds, an excellent specimen embodying perhaps all the selective breeding lavished on the native bantam over many years.

Rosecombs are small and cobby but sprightly and males have one sweeping curve from neck to tail. Their head features make them particularly striking, but they are not easy to preserve for show as their combs easily become scratched and scarred and their lobes blistered. The black variety is particularly popular, followed by white and blue versions, although a further number of additional colours are beginning to appear after emerging in Germany and Holland.

If you want to purchase stock cheaply or are more concerned with high egg production and good food to egg ratio, you may want to consider the hybrid varieties. The advantages are that they are readily available, cheap to purchase, easily replaced, and will produce lots of eggs for the first two years. The disadvantage is that you will not be able to reproduce them (cockerels are rarely sold), your surplus stock has little or no value, and you cannot claim to have 'pedigree' birds or that you are doing your bit for the conservation effort!

The commercially available hybrids are given catchy names in an effort to grab your attention and to sound like pure breeds. Certainly, in some smallholding magazines they are advertised as if they are pure breeds which is misleading.

Small is Beautiful

Quite frequently domestic poultry keepers specialise in the Lilliputian breeds of poultry called bantams. These little hens take up only a small amount of space and are certainly economical to feed. The egg they lay is smaller, but bantam eggs are great favourites with the children.

It is generally thought that the original bantams came from Java. These perky little birds have a different action in walking from that of the standard hen – a kind of jerky gait which gives them a jaunty manner. It is, however, a mistake to think that bantams can be kept more easily than larger breeds of poultry. In fact, the opposite is true since in some respects bantams require more attention than large fowls, especially if they are kept for exhibition, and they are more prone to colds.

Bantam fowl eat only about half the quantity of food needed by a standard hen, but neither do they give so many eggs. They average about 100 eggs a year, although individual strains of bantam have laid as many as 175 eggs per bird each year.

There are bantams of most varieties of full-sized poultry, including Rhode Island Red bantams and a scaled-down version of that famous old breed the Plymouth Rock.

A suitable house for six bantams need be no larger than 4 feet 6 inches (1.5 m) long by about 3 feet (1 m) wide, with a height of just under 3 feet (1 m) in front, sloping 4 inches (90 mm) to the back. To this house attach a run about 9 feet (3 m) long and the same width.

Popular Game Birds

If there is one breed of fowl that belongs to England more than any other, it is the game fowl. At the time of the Roman occupation of our land it is recorded that the Britons kept fowls 'for pleasure and diversion' and although the breed is not specifically mentioned, or the sport defined, no doubt the historian was referring to cock fighting. Some of the earliest Chinese records also mention cock fighting, while in India there are references going back to 1000 BC.

Today, game birds are among the most popular of all bantam type poultry. They have a large number of admirers and, like all bantams, make interesting birds for the family poultry keeper whether he exhibits at shows or not.

Apart from their historical association with the now banned cock fighting, game fowl have provided the small poultry fancier with a fascinating hobby and the best materials with which to try his skill at breeding for exhibition purposes.

Game fowls are divided into two classes – Old English and Modern. Both are composed of many varieties, each named according to the colour of its plumage. Modern game fowl mainly owe their origin to the warriors of the old-time cockpits and are characterised by their long legs and heads and shortness of feather. It was, however, devoid of economic utility qualities and the fanciers turned to the more useful Old English type of fowl (see Fig. 72) – the perfect combination of the useful and beautiful in bird life.

Game birds lay white shelled eggs which, although a little below average in size, are unequalled for fullness of yolk and richness of flavour.

Fig. 72 The Old English Game Spangled Cock

Ducks

Ducks may be kept so economically and give such a good return, that many domestic (and commercial) poultrymen prefer them to fowls.

Ducks are the cheapest form of livestock to house and if you keep a laying breed such as the Khaki Campbell (as distinct from a table breed like the well-known white Aylesbury) they lay more eggs than fowls – particularly so in the second year of production (as many as 300 eggs a year is not uncommon). Kept as **table** birds, ducks attain killing size much quicker than chickens – at 10 weeks an Aylesbury can weigh at least 5 lbs (2 kilos) and they can be fed very largely on potatoes and greenstuff.

There is just one snag for the domestic keeper: ducks are not recommended for small back gardens in built-up areas – their quacking and the quagmire they make of a small run in wet weather are serious disadvantages. But if your house stands in the open and has a large garden, or access to a field or grass run, as many village properties do, then ducks are both profitable and a joy to own. Swimming water is not necessary unless you keep ducks for breeding, when a pond is desirable if the ducks are to mate successfully and ensure good fertility.

Housing for Ducks

You may hear it said that ducks can live an entirely open air life. Maybe, but the best results by far are obtained (with both laying and table ducks) by housing the birds at night and also making sure the ducks have daytime shelter from hot, summer sun by providing enough shade from trees and shrubs. Certainly the housing for ducks is far less elaborate than that needed for hens. There is no need for a house with glass windows and other fittings; all ducks need is a dry, well-ventilated house giving them around 4 to 5 sq feet (.5 sq m) of floor space each – so a simple house 4 feet 6 inches (1.5 m) long by 4 feet (1.25 m) wide will provide very ample room for a flock of 10 ducks. Such a house need only be about 4 feet (1.25 m) high at the front and just under 1 yard (1 m) at the back – ducks do not perch, as hens do, and this is why the structure does not need to be as high as a hen house.

A slatted wooden floor, which helps to keep the litter dry, should be fitted to the ducks' house and raised about 2 inches (5 cm) off the base. The upper 1 foot (.3 m) of the front should be filled in with wire netting, protected by an overlaying weatherboard.

Make the whole front loose, or on hinges, so that it can be removed bodily, or opened, in warm weather.

Ducks are clumsy creatures, so do give them a sloping run-up board into the house otherwise if they have to jump to get inside they will injure themselves. Nest boxes are simple affairs of straw on the floor, kept in position either with a few bricks or some shallow planks of wood.

If possible, face a duck house towards the south-east, south or south-west to get all the sun possible and have a small run attached – this is because ducks should be kept penned up till about 10 am, by which time eggs will have been laid in the house instead of wasting your time searching the grounds later in the day.

Feeding

As much as three-quarters of a duck's daily food ration can consist of vegetable matter. Cooked potatoes, carrots and swedes are the mainstay and these should be mixed with water and dry mash (obtainable, like layers' mash for hens, from farmers) to form a fairly sloppy but appetising meal. Two meals a day should be given, allowing each duck a little over 4 oz 100 g).

As with hens, supplies of water, grit and oyster shell must always be available for ducks. Although swimming water is not essential for a domestic flock of ducks kept only for meat or egg production, to stay healthy they must have water deep enough to immerse their entire head.

If your ducks are to average 300 eggs a year – and this should be your target per bird – they must be well looked after even though the labour required is ridiculously small for such a hefty return.

Routine work consists of loosening up the floor litter **every** morning and changing the litter as soon as it becomes wet through and foul. While straw will last only a couple of weeks before it needs changing, peat moss litter will last **two months** if kept raked over.

Ducks do not like fierce winds – egg yield can be cut by a third if the birds lack shelter. A hedge, a row of trees, a clump of shrubs, a range of buildings are all satisfactory places for shelter – and if you cannot manage any of these then a few sheets of corrugated iron placed lengthways will serve the purpose.

Above all, remember that these delightful birds respond to tranquillity in every way. They need quiet and gentle handling, and a move to a different house – or a change of feeding – when ducks have begun winter laying will not only reduce egg yields but probably put some into partial moult.

Rearing Ducklings

Ducklings is the term applied to young ducks and drakes. They can, like chickens, be reared either by natural or artificial means.

By broody hen: Make a comfortable nest on a sod of turf – remembering to moisten around the nest in very warm or dry weather, since duck eggs require more moisture than hen's eggs. During the 28 days needed for incubation manage the 'mother hen' just as described for hatching chickens under a broody.

By brooder: Ducklings need a little less heat than chickens, and any ordinary good brooder (as described on page 44) will rear ducklings, but the litter beneath the brooder will need changing frequently as it speedily becomes soaked through. Up to the third day ducklings need to be watched closely to make sure they know, after wandering about, where to go back for warmth (they can be annoyingly stupid little creatures!).

Picking out the best layers is as important with ducks as with hens. Feeding stuffs are too dear to waste on below-average birds – so learn to know the characteristics of the good laying duck; she is active, first at the food container and last away, and is early 'about the house' in the mornings and late to 'get into bed' at night!

Another sign of a prolific layer is the

Fig. 73 Water fowl breeds

appearance of being nice and plump behind and walking with that typical duck manner of legs wide apart, The good duck is all curves; an angular looking bird is a doubtful layer.

Breeds to Keep _____

It is generally agreed that all domestic ducks (with the exception of the Muscovy from South America) are descended from the wild duck or Mallard.

The following are the most important of the very large number of different breeds of domestic duck:

Aylesbury: This duck (Fig. 74), originating

from the Vale of Aylesbury, rightly occupies the top position among birds bred for the table. Its popularity stems from its ability to attain size and weight at a very early age – good alike for the early duckling trade and the

Fig. 74 The Aylesbury

home food producer. Quality and flavour of flesh is excellent. Lays a large bluish-green egg and has glossy, pure white plumage.

Khaki-Campbell: Developed from the original bird named after a certain Mrs Campbell who crossed an Indian Runner (her particular bird laid 182 eggs in 196 days!) with one of a very hardy Rouen breed. The modern Khaki-Campbell is **the** outstanding egg layer, frequently giving 300 white eggs in one year. Plumage of the drakes is khaki colour all over, except for bronze-green head and stern; the ducks are entirely khaki colour with a few feathers of lighter shade on back and wings.

Fig. 75 The Khaki-Campbell

Indian Runner: Formerly classed as the best egg laying breed of duck. There are five varieties – black, chocolate, fawn, fawn and white, and white.

Of Indian origin, this breed was introduced into the county of Cumberland about 100 years ago. The bird is of a different formation from other ducks – with a high and erect shape to its body and a flat skull. Eggs are medium-sized and white.

Cayuga: Not as popular as it should be, considering the breed combines good laying and table qualities. These birds are a deep greenish-black in colour and have also been known as the Black Duck of North America (it is noteworthy that a lake in North America bears the name Cayuga and black coloured duck abound there).

The shape of the Cayuga duck is like that of the Aylesbury, but its eggs are dark green.

Rouen: A complete contrast in egg colour from the breed mentioned above – the Rouen lays a blue egg. It is an excellent table bird, often crossed with the Aylesbury. The Rouen's plumage is very like that of the lovely wild Mallard (the reason why so many of the breed are seen on ornamental waters) and the Rouen male undergoes the same peculiar changes in summer when the drake's beautiful bottle-green head and brownish-red markings are lost in the moult and he becomes nearly indistinguishable from the drabber, brown-mottled duck.

Pekin: Imported from China in the 19th century, this excellent table bird is second only to the Aylesbury, and as a layer of eggs it is **better** than the latter – hence Aylesbury and Pekins are often crossed. The Pekin breed of duck is

Fig. 76 The Pekin

Fig. 77 White Call ducks

very hardy and a thrifty forager for food. The colour is a uniform cream throughout, with bright orange bill, shanks and feet. Pekins lay a blue egg.

Orpington: For some years, when the rage for buff colour in all poultry was at its height, these ducks enjoyed a considerable vogue but they are less popular today. However, they are a useful dual purpose breed ideal for limited space. Orpingtons make very presentable ducklings, to eat or to sell, at eight to 10 weeks and laying qualities are above average for a recognised table breed.

Colour of this breed is either buff or blue and white. They are excellent free range birds, and they lay a white egg.

Call: The Call (Fig. 78) has been known in Holland for many centuries but originally evolved in the East Indies. Certainly, they are the number-one domestic breed of duck on the continent, and the most popular in Britain. Classified as a bantam duck, and tiny in comparison to other ducks, they are very sociable, easy to breed, and particularly good for children. There are numerous colours of Call, but without doubt the most frequently seen is the White (Fig. 77) which, when presented in top form, always seems to be amongst the prizes. The Call will not lay huge numbers of eggs but the females do make very good mothers.

Fig. 78 A charming Call duck female of the apricot colour. Call ducks are a tiny breed with massive popularity.

Geese

Geese can be a very useful addition to the poultry keeper's flock. However, due to their size, life span, and the occasionally 'aggressive' nature of the males (in reality, this is protectiveness towards his mate or young), some careful thought and planning is required before you decide to obtain stock.

Geese will not bite or attack unless provoked but will be very protective of their young in Spring. They have been known to attack dogs, apparently mistaking them for a fox. Whilst consideration needs to be given to young children, generally such attacks are not repeated – the animal in question usually learns to keep its distance!

Geese can become very good pets, are very good at grazing and keeping slugs and snails at bay, and are often a good alternative to guard dogs given the noise they make to announce the arrival of strangers. They do however live longer than other poultry, often well into their 'teens'.

It is advisable for a beginner to start with a pair or trio of adult geese or goslings and confine them to a movable pen until the birds become accustomed to their new situation. A movable pen allows the geese to be changed to fresh pasture. Many keepers prefer to house their geese in a permanent house and allow them to free range. This situation is ideal. Whilst security should be given against foxes and other predators, domestic geese don't need much for housing. They do require shelter from the worst weather and wind. Some people just make a 2 bale high 'U' of hay bales and cover this with plywood, facing the opening towards the south. Also consider that the domestic breeds of geese are not capable of flight, although with a tail wind and a running start they can sometimes clear a 4-5 foot fence, especially if it's downhill.

Once fully grown, geese do not need the same amount of protein as fowl and turkeys. Grain – with wheat being a good option – should be the basis of their diet. Geese love to forage and root around on free range and find titbits. They are not vegetarian and will eat slugs, snails, worms, froglets, and small rodents. They will also enjoy all fruit and vegetable waste.

Goose eggs take 30 days to hatch. The goslings can be raised in much the same fashion as ducklings. They are quite hardy and will not require heat after a month, particularly in warm weather. Many people choose to raise goslings naturally – the adults make excellent parents and the females will readily go broody. A nest box is required for each breeding pair of geese.

Breeds of domestic geese are generally classified into one of three groupings according to size and weight, namely: light, medium, and heavy. Breeds within the first two categories are best if you do not have deep water and want to breed from your stock. The light breeds will all mate successfully without water in which to swim and the medium varieties can mate in relatively shallow water. The larger heavy breeds of geese need considerable amounts of water. They often prefer to pair rather than live in groups and need grazing and often supplementary greens to vary the diet. The heavy breeds have a particularly long life span and many will not breed until at least two years old.

Popular Geese Breeds

Chinese geese, a light breed, are smaller than others and distinguishable from other geese by the knob or protuberance on the head. Two colour varieties are known: the white, and the brown-grey. Chinese geese go broody easily and are generally better layers, producing 50-100 eggs per season. Chinese are the most suitable 'watchdog' geese with a curiosity unrivalled by other breeds. They are also ideal for crossing with other breeds, having a better bone/meat ratio than the others and a leaner carcass with little or no fat.

The white Roman goose, another light breed, was imported from Italy in around 1903. Early birds often appeared with grey markings on their backs and a few will show this defect today. They are very compact chubby birds with no keel, their distinctive feature is their short neck and shorter back/body line. The variety is particularly popular in the USA and Europe as the basis for a small eating goose with a good meat to bone ratio and being prolific breeders. Their most distinctive feature is their short neck and shorter back/body line.

The uniquely plumaged Sebastopol (Fig. 79) – a light breed – originated in Europe. Their distinctive frizzled feathers curl due to the lack of a rigid feather spine/quill. Many people keep them for their ornamental qualities. They are average layers as a breed and can be short. They are unable to even attempt to fly having no true wings and they do need some extra care from adverse environmental conditions and plentiful water in order to groom and care for their plumage.

The Pomeranian is arguably the best of the medium varieties and was originally created to brave the colder winters of northern Germany. Even now, the breed is particularly hardy. An excellent foraging breed which requires a good supply of green food to thrive. Varieties include white, grey, and saddleback. Annual egg production is usually around 30 eggs per bird. The females are particularly good mothers.

Fig. 79 A Sebastopol goose with its unique curled feathering. As this photo shows, geese can become very friendly.

The **Toulouse** is one of the largest heavy goose breeds and a good choice for the smallholder. In its 'dewlap' form, the Toulouse may weigh 25 lbs with its body barely clearing the floor. Originally bred in southern France for pâté de foie gras, the breed is widely considered to be the superior meat bird in Europe. Although a heavy variety, the Toulouse does well in confinement as their size restricts foraging. Nevertheless they are adept layers, usually averaging 40 eggs per bird with 60 not unknown.

Turkeys

Turkeys have enjoyed increasing popularity over the last few years, particularly in the UK where the upturn in interest has lead to the formation of a specialist club. One factor has been the popularity of organic produce – keeping turkeys offers the possibility of a flavoursome roast on the table with no shortage of outlets for surplus stock.

Turkeys may require slightly more room than chickens – it is vital not to overcrowd them – and need a little more care when young or if breeding but other than that should not be feared by the prospective keeper. Rather, they present an attractive option with a wide range of colours, a striking feature in a garden, smallholding, or farmyard, and can become very tame making good pets.

Turkeys can be housed in much the same way as chickens. Certainly the principles outlined earlier should be followed. Some Turkey keepers favour a veranda housing system which allows birds to go outside the house into a wire veranda (sometimes roofed) for fresh air and sunlight. The veranda can be attached to the house via a pop-hole. Others prefer to allow the birds to free range in good weather, keeping them inside during rain. Like other types of poultry turkeys can tolerate cold providing they have access to a dry and draught-free area.

Turkeys will naturally perch on the highest suitable roost. However, high roosts are not to be encouraged because frequently the turkeys bruise themselves, and even break wings, when flying down from great heights. Under intensive conditions of housing some farmers do not provide perches, but allow the turkeys to roost on the litter. This system apparently works well in some situations, but is not generally advisable.

Periodic handling is necessary for a variety of reasons, including checking the condition of the birds, noting whether external parasites are becoming troublesome, in order to isolate birds that may have become damaged by the males (stags), and to remove birds that are unhealthy in any way.

Choosing Your Turkeys

Although there are nowhere near the same number of different varieties of turkeys as in chickens, they do provide the prospective keeper with a wide choice of colour.

The older breeds tend to do better outside than the commercial strains; they are very hardy, totally impervious to the cold preferring to roost outside and if it has been frosty you can hear the feathers crackle as they jump down in the morning. They like some protection from the wet and wind, like most birds, and somewhere quite dark to lay their eggs which they will incubate and rear successfully. They are susceptible to the fox, so protection from vermin is important.

Bronze is the colour of turkey most similar to the wild turkey 'Meleagris gallopavo' which is still hunted in North and South America and from which all domestic colours are derived. The turkey is said to have arrived in Europe around the 16th century and has been domesticated ever since.

The **White** has been developed for the meat trade as it plucks clean and free from dark feather stubs. The growing potential of the commercial strains of Whites is fantastic and has been developed for the greater proportion of breast meat to leg meat than ever the older coloured turkeys will have. The fashion has come full circle recently as the bronze is back in favour with the dark feather stubs as proof that it is a bronze and therefore carrying a price premium.

Other colours of turkey vary widely: the **Norfolk Black** was the favourite for meat in the Eastern Counties for many years: the **Buff** is probably the rarest colour, it is a lovely rich shade of gingery brown with white wings and tail; the **Pied** (**Crollwitzer** in Germany, **Royal Palm** in USA) is an attractive contrast of black and white stripes; the **Blue** is a delicate lavender and the **Slate** rather darker. Colours developed in America include the **Narragansett** (brown, grey and black), the **Nebraskan spotted** (buff, black and white freckled) and the **Bourbon Red** which is a burgundy contrasted with white.

Breeding

The breeding turkeys must be handled at regular intervals throughout the breeding season, and in order to facilitate this it is advisable to make special arrangements for catching the birds. If it is difficult to handle the turkeys, there is a tendency for the job to be missed out.

Ample nest-box accommodation is required at all times during the breeding season and particularly during periods of very hot weather. There should be sufficient nesting space so that from one-third to one-half of the birds may lay at any one time. If insufficient nesting accommodation is provided, the turkeys will crowd into the nests and some may be suffocated and eggs broken.

As with other varieties of poultry, turkey hens will become broody. Broody turkeys should be confined to an airy and well-ventilated - but not draughty - coop as soon as possible after it is known that the birds are broody. It is a good idea to check the nest boxes every evening during the breeding season. Occasionally mistakes will be made, but generally this routine will ensure that all the hens are placed in the coops on the first occasion that they desire to spend a night on the nest.

The broody hens should be confined for from four to five days, and during this time they should be fed on a breeders' diet in the same manner as the remaining birds in the flocks. The aim is to stimulate the ovary into production. The idea that grain feeding is best during the broody stage is quite wrong, for this may tend to throw the bird out of lay. Lack of attention to broodies can soon lead to a fall in egg production, thus valuable hatching eggs are lost.

It is often rather difficult to be certain that birds really are broody, but if every bird is placed in the broody coop whenever it appears to wish to remain on the nest at night, then few mistakes will be made. Unlike hens, turkeys do not cluck when they first become broody. However, they may be heard to hiss and there is a tendency for them to walk on tiptoes.

Young turkey chicks and poults require much the same treatment as their fowl counterparts although they often behave in a near-suicidal manner. This makes it important to make sure they cannot drown in drinking water or become isolated from a heat source. The youngsters also need a higher protein provision in their feed.

Feeding Breeding Stock _____

Breeding turkeys require a very highly digestible diet and one that contains all the nutrients for high hatchability. The form in which the food is presented to the turkeys is not of great importance and specially prepared turkey breeder pellets are ideal. It is important, however, to ensure that the nutrients for high hatchability are always present in the total diet in sufficient quantity. Unless this precaution is taken, it may well be that egg production will be satisfactory but that many of the eggs will fail to hatch. The presence of adequate manganese, riboflavin and so-called animal protein complex are essential for good results.

Nutrition is the undoing of many turkey keepers, and every year large numbers of eggs fail to hatch simply because insufficient attention has been given to balancing the diet. Where purchased foods are used, then the merchant should be asked to supply mixtures that are suitable for turkey breeding stock. Mixtures designed for chickens are not always suitable.

Know Your Law

Some basic knowledge of the law, as it touches on livestock keeping, is always worth having.

Trespass: poultry are proverbial trespassers and often the source of friction between neighbours. The law says that owners must keep their animals on their own land and if they do not do so they will be liable to compensate neighbours for any damage done. So, if your poultry are not properly fenced in and they enter your neighbour's garden and ruin his immaculate seed bed, scratch out his prize potted plants or peck his fruit then **you** will be liable because you neglected to perform your duty of providing adequate fencing-in.

A mistake frequently made is to believe that the owner of a fence dividing two properties is responsible for keeping and maintaining the fence in such condition as to make trespass impossible. It is true that in certain cases fence owners are under what is called a 'prescriptive obligation' to maintain the fence for their neighbour's benefit but there is never any such obligation where **poultry** is concerned.

Supposing the worst has happened and your neighbour is irate owing to your poultry being in his garden - in order to obtain **damages** your neighbour must furnish **proof** both of the accuracy of his costing of damage done and **proof** that this damage was, in fact, caused by your poultry not being properly fenced in.

If the poultry keeper can show that he had taken 'all reasonable precautions' and that it was by reason of some **third party's act** that the fowls escaped (someone leaving a gate open, for instance), he would not be liable. For the neighbour to obtain an injunction it would be necessary for him to demonstrate that you, the poultry keeper, threaten or intend a repetition of the trespass, or that there is reason to fear that it will happen again.

Unlike ducks and geese, hens have no right of way on the road. If a motorist kills them he is not obliged to pay.

Dogs and Cats: of particular interest to poultry keepers is the question of damage to poultry by dogs and cats.

Here the poultry owner is covered in the same way as a farmer and his livestock where liabilities are imposed on the owner of a dog for injuries done to cattle. In proven cases of other people's pets injuring, or even killing, your poultry, compensation is recoverable.

Law of Nuisances: by law there are several ways in which poultry might land you in trouble as a nuisance. Trespass (see above) is a nuisance – as is cock crowing or the keeping of poultry under insanitary conditions.

Cock crowing is not an offence against any particular Act of Parliament, but against local bylaws which, in fact, have the same effect. Some local authorities have bylaws declaring that 'cattle, dogs and poultry shall not be kept in such places or in such manner as to be a nuisance or annoyance to the inhabitants'.

Insanitary Conditions: all alleged nuisances under this heading can be dealt with under the Public Health Acts. Complaint about your poultry must first be lodged to the local authority. If satisfied with the genuineness of the complaint they will serve notice on the poultry keeper to stop the nuisance within a certain time – or be taken to court.

Cruelty: as with other livestock reared for human consumption, poultry have to be killed for food and no offence of cruelty is committed unless the killing is accompanied by inflicting unnecessary suffering. The newcomer to poultry keeping can study the leaflets on this and other aspects of domestic poultry keeping issued by the Royal Society for the Prevention of Cruelty to Animals (send a stamped and addressed envelope to the Society at Wilberforce Way, Southwater, Horsham, W. Sussex RH13 9RS. tel. 0870 335 999).

Glossary of Poultry Terms

Air Cell Air space usually found in the large end of the egg.

Albumen The white of the egg.

American Breeds Those breeds developed in America and having common characteristics such as yellow skin, non-feathered shanks, red ear lobes.

Axial Feather The short wing feather between the primaries and secondaries.

Baby Chick Newly hatched chick before it has been fed or watered.

Bantam Diminutive fowl. Some are distinct breeds, others are miniatures of large breeds.

Barring Alternate stripes of light and dark across a feather, most distinctly seen in the Barred Plymouth Rock breed.

Beak Upper and lower mandibles of chickens, turkeys, pheasants, pea fowl, etc.

Bean Hard protuberance on the upper mandible of water fowl.

Beard A bunch of feathers under the throat of some fowls, such as Faverolles, Houdans and certain varieties of Polands.

Bill The upper and lower mandibles of waterfowl.

Blood Spot Blood in an egg caused by a rupture of small blood vessels usually at the time of ovulation.

Boots Feathers projecting from the toes, as in the Brahma and Cochin breeds.

Breast The forward part of the body between the neck and the keel bone.

Breed A group of fowl related by ancestry and breeding true to certain characteristics such as body shape and size.

Broiler Young chickens under 9 weeks of age of either sex, that are tender-meated with soft, pliable, smooth-textured skin.

Brooder Heat source for starting young birds.

Broody Maternal instinct causing the female to want to hatch eggs.

Candle To determine the interior quality of an egg through the use of a special light in a dark room.

Cannibalism The habit of eating other birds in the flock.

Cap A comb; also the back part of a fowl's skull.

Cape The feathers under and at the base of the neck-hackle, between the shoulders.

Capon A male fowl treated with a female hormone to produce better quality table birds.

Cock A male bird over 12 months of age.

Cockerel A male bird under 12 months of age.

Comb The fleshy prominence on the top of the head of fowl.

Crest A crown or tuft of feathers on the head; sometimes called the 'top-knot' and known in Old English Game as the 'tassel'.

Crop An enlargement of the gullet where food is stored and prepared for digestion.

Crossbred The first generation resulting from crossing two different breeds or varieties.

Cull A bird not suitable to be in a laying or breeding pen.

Culling Removing unsuitable birds from the flock.

Debeak To remove a part of the beak to prevent feather pulling or cannibalism.

Drake Male duck.

Dub To trim the comb and wattles close to the head.

Ear Lobe Fleshy patch of skin below ear. It may be red, white, blue or purple, depending upon the breed.

Embryo The young organism in the early stages of development, before hatching from the egg.

Face Skin around and below the eyes.

Flight Feathers Primary feathers of the wing, sometimes used to denote the primaries and secondaries.

Fowl Term applied collectively to chickens, ducks, geese, etc. or the market class designation for old laying birds.

Gander Male goose.

Germinal Disc or **Blastodisc** Site of fertilisation on the egg yolk.

Gizzard Muscular stomach. Its main function is grinding food and partial digestion of proteins.

Goose The female goose as distinguished from the gander.

Gosling A young goose of either sex.

Gullet or **Oesophagus** The tubular structure leading from the mouth to the glandular stomach.

Hackle Plumage on the side and rear of the neck of fowl.

Hen A female fowl more than 12 months of age.

Hock The joint of the leg between the lower thigh and the shank.

Horn Term used to describe various colour shadings in the beak of some breeds of fowl such as the Rhode Island Red.

Hover Canopy used on brooder stoves to hold heat near the floor when brooding young stock.

Isthmus Part of the oviduct where the shell membranes are added during egg formation.

Keel Bone Breast bone or sternum.

Laced, Lacing A stripe or edging all round a feather, differing in colour from the rest of the feather.

Leg Feathers Feathers projecting from the outer sides of the legs, of such breeds as Brahmas, Cochins and other fanciers' breeds.

Litter Soft, absorbent material used to cover floors of poultry houses.

Magnum Part of the oviduct which secretes the thick albumen or white during the process of egg formation.

Mandible The upper or lower bony portion of the beak.

Marking The barring, lacing, pencilling, spangling, etc. of the plumage.

Moult To shed old feathers and regrow new ones.

Mossy Confused or indistinct marking: A defect.

Muffing The beard (as in Faverolles, for instance) and the whiskers, i.e. the whole of the head feathering except the crest.

Oil Sac (Uropygial Gland) Large oil gland on the back at the base of the tail-used to preen or condition the feathers.

Ova Round bodics (yolks) attached to the ovary. These drop into oviduct and become yolk of the egg.

Oviduct Long glandular tube where egg formation takes place and leading from the ovary to the cloaca. It is made up of the funnel, magnum, isthmus, uterus and vagina.

Pencilling Small markings or stripes over a feather – straight across in Hamburgh hens, and often known as bands.

Pendulous Crop Crop that is usually impacted and enlarged and hangs down in an abnormal manner.

Perch A wooden pole on which fowl rest or sleep.

Plumage The feathers making up the outer covering of fowls.

Poult A young turkey.

Poultry A term designating those species of birds which are used by man for food and fibre and can be reproduced under his care. The term includes chickens, turkeys, ducks, waterfowl, pheasants, pigeons, peafowl, guineas and ostriches.

Primaries The long stiff flight feathers at the outer tip of the wing.

Pubic Bones The thin terminal portion of the hip bones that form part of the pelvis. Are used as an aid in judging productivity of laying birds.

Pullet Female chicken less than 1 year of age.

Recycle, or **Force Moult** To force into a moult with a cessation of egg production.

Replacements Young birds which will replace an old flock.

Roasters Chickens of either sex, usually 3 to 5 months of age.

Roosting Fowl at rest or sleeping.

Rose Comb A broad, solid comb, nearly flat on top, covered with several small regular points and finishing with a spike. Seen very well in the Redcap breed, long familiar in Derbyshire and South Yorkshire.

Saddle Lower part of the back.

Secondaries The large wing feathers adjacent to the body, visible when the wing is folded or extended.

Sex-Linked Any inherited factor linked to the sex chromosomes of either parent. Plumage colour differences between the male and female progeny of some crosses is an example of sex-linkage. Useful in day old sexing of chicks.

Shank Leg.

Shell Membranes The two membranes attached to the inner egg shell. They normally separate at the large end of the egg to form air cells.

Sickles The long, curved feathers of a cock's tail.

Snood Fleshy appendage on the head of a turkey.

Spangling The marking produced by a large spot of colour on each feather differing from that of the ground colour.

Spur The stiff, horny projection on the legs of some birds. Found on the inner side of the shanks.

Strain Fowl of any breed usually with a given breeder's name and which has been reproduced by closed-flock breeding for several generations.

Tail Coverts Soft, curved feathers at the sides of the lower part of the tail.

Tail Feathers Straight and stiff feathers of the tail only. (In the male fowl the tail feathers are contained inside the sickles and coverts.)

Testes The male sex glands.

Thigh That part of the leg above the shank.

Tom A male turkey.

'Top-Knot' (See Crest.)

Trachea or **Windpipe** That part of the respiratory system that conveys air from the larynx to the bronchi and to the lungs.

Under colour Colour of the downy part of the plumage.

Uterus The portion of the oviduct where the thin white, the shell and shell pigment are added during egg formation.

Vagina Section of the oviduct which holds the formed egg until it is laid.

Variety A sub-division of breed – distinguished either by colour, pattern or comb type.

Vent The external opening, the anus.

Wattles The thin pendant appendages at either side of the base of the beak and upper throat, usually much larger in males than in females.

Wry Tail A tail carried awry, to either side of the continuation of the backbone.

Yolk Ovum, the yellow portion of the egg.

Useful Addresses

British Waterfowl Association
Rachel Boer, Secretary
Oaklands
Blind Lane
Tanworth in Arden
Solihull
B94 5HS
Website: www.waterfowl.org.uk

The BWA is an association of enthusiasts interested in keeping, breeding and conserving all kinds of waterfowl including wildfowl, domestic ducks and geese. It holds its own Championship Show and many other events throughout the year.

Fancy Fowl Magazine
Barn Acre House
Saxted Green
Woodbridge
Suffolk
IP13 9QJ

A monthly publication covering fancy and utility poultry keeping.

Paul Chapman Illustrations
Old Bell Farm
Billingford
Dereham
Norfolk
NR20 4RF

Poultry Planet
Email: info@poultryplanet.com
www.poultryplanet.com

Poultry Planet is one of the largest poultry websites in the world and offers members and non-members a wide range of poultry services. It provides contact information for organisations around the world and is very useful for finding sources of stock.

The National Federation of Poultry Clubs
A D Keep, Secretary
Riverlea, 11 Oakley Road
Clapham
Bedford
MK41 6AN
Website: www.nfpc.org.uk

The NFPC's main function is to organise the biggest poultry show in the country held at Stafford, the Federation Show (December), which includes a sale section.

The Poultry Club of Great Britain
Mike Clark, Secretary
30 Grovesnor Road, Frampton, Boston,
Lincolnshire
PE20 1DB
Website: www.poultryclub.org

The Poultry Club is responsible for the official poultry standards and organises the Nation Championship Show (December), judgin exams, and is the umbrella organisation for specific breed clubs.

The Turkey Club UK
J Houghton-Wallace, Secretary
'Graycots', 4 Kingston Road
Great Eversden
Cambridge
CB3 7HT

For anyone interested in Turkeys.

Index